BA GUA QUAN
Eight Trigrams Boxing

ESSENTIAL GUIDE

Dr. Michael Guen

Other works by Michael Guen:

Eight Standing Meditations videotape and DVD ©Wasah Institute

Yin Fu Ba Gua Quan (Eight Trigrams Boxing): Study Manual and Curriculum

Yin Fu Ba Gua Quan: Eight Lesson Primer

Ba Gua Quan—Eight Trigrams Fist: Pao Chui and Practical Applications (Yin Fu Ba Gua Series, Book 2)

Ba Gua Zhang—Eight Trigrams Palm: Eight Mother Palms, Eight Standing Meditations, Eight Palm Fist, and Practical Applications (Yin Fu Ba Gua Series, Book 3)

For further information, contact Dr. Michael Guen:
Email: michael@guensystem.com
Web site: www.guensystem.com

Published by Wasah Institute
Santa Rosa, California USA

ISBN 0-9709664-3-1

Grand Master Gong Baozai and the author in 1992. He was eighty-eight years old when this photograph was taken.

In honor of all of those who were
required to learn under the severe conditions
of the “Cloak and Bowl Descendant” system.
Their sacrifices preserved a sacred tradition
so that eternal truths could later be made
available to the entire world community.

Acknowledgements

This book is dedicated to those who participated in the early years of the American-based lineage. Their commitment and sacrifices, which led to reworking of the community structure of the tradition, have made the teachings available for future generations.

I am indebted to David Finks for helping initiate this project and writing the first edition with me.

My heartfelt thanks go to Patricia Bernard, George Bernard, and Katie McKee, whose unwavering faith and support since the beginning of the American work has provided inspiration for this project.

Finally, my gratitude to Leo Guen, Jean O'Connor, and Art Buehler for proofreading and critical commentary, and to Mali Apple for offering her editorial expertise to bring this work into completed form.

Contents

Preface

In the old days, it would have been an act of betrayal to reveal the role character relationships play in the attainment of total mastery. The vital dynamics of the master-disciple and disciple-disciple relationships were kept hidden. All that was publicly taught were ritualized forms and techniques. The full framework of a system was intentionally kept secret. The degree of trust and intimacy between master and disciple was the greatest factor determining how much of a master's transmission was to be conveyed.

In the past century, with the opening of previously closed societies to outside cultures and influences, the standards of many authentic teachings have become compromised or lost. This work discloses detailed elements of character relationships within the curriculum of Grand Master Gong Baozai's transmission. Preservation of the orthodox standard of character is vital for successful adaptation of ancient life-practice systems in these modern, multicultural times.

Introduction

In his teachings, Gong Baozai revealed to me that *character* was more than just external performance. I had been under the assumption that he was referring to an interpretation in which to be an upstanding individual entailed blind obedience and robotic conformity. In fact, he introduced an idea I had never heard, wherein *proper* character necessitates expression of personal courage, authenticity, and creativity.

Rather than a suppressive prohibiting force, Gong Baozai's interpretation of character offers the seeker a unique brand of protection from the evil forces of the world. Providing access to inner life skills and resources, adaptability is optimized as the objective elements of one's life practice comes alive in principled thoughts, words, and actions.

My own lessons in this respect came slowly and painfully. After ten years of relentless martial art training, I collapsed. Driving ambition and its companion—reckless disregard toward self and others—led to a physical and emotional breakdown, forcing me to reassess my basic motives for practice. This setback sparked a radical shift in my perspective. Sickness and emotional suffering brought me face to face with my own callous insensitivity, opening me to a hidden aspect of the ba gua quan transmission that Gong Baozai had all along tried to convey. I was finally able to understand the essential role character training and community relationships play on the road to martial arts mastery.

From the orthodox standpoint, character is defined broadly. While social harmony and basic conformity is advocated, conduct must moreover foster a deepening relationship between one's inner and outer worlds, in its myriad dimensions. Each new experience one has, if properly examined and integrated, increases the ability to use ordinary daily life as a tool for clarification and fulfillment of one's destiny.

Like a parent with a child, a teacher's effort to mold well-rounded character in students is a largely unacknowledged yet precious gift. Character is the real key to withstanding the stringent demands of higher learning, while remaining inwardly peaceful and content.

How to use this book

In two other works, *Ba Gua Quan: Eight Trigrams Fist* and *Ba Gua Zhang: Eight Trigrams Palm,* I present elements of the physical framework within which character can be cultivated. However, without spiritual guidance that elevates the mind beyond the mundane, even specialized methods such as ba gua quan will produce little more than a shell.

To this end, the *Essential Guide* offers two distinct learning tracks. Through philosophical discourse, Part I espouses the "inner principles" of character. The writing style in Part I is deliberately succinct. My intention is to impart to the reader an experience similar in tightness and rigor to the process I underwent while endlessly pouring over classical Chinese material with Gong Baozai. He would use simple terms, yet the implications ran to boundless depths. In a classroom setting, one or two paragraphs could be read at a time, allowing a period afterward for contemplation and discussion. This way, the proper mood of the tradition may be sufficiently conveyed.

Through illustration of foundation movements and postures, Part 2 explores the "inner mechanics" of character. Inner and outer elements in communication make unification of the entire human possible. Such is the deepest revelation set forth by the wise ancients that make all martial art systems one.

Michael Guen
Santa Rosa, California
January 2005

Part I

The Spirit of Ba Gua Quan

The ancients knew that it is not the body that rules the mind, but that the body follows the command of the mind. A primary aim of higher learning, above and beyond molding and training the physical body, is thus to rectify the thinking and beliefs. In Gong Baozai's teaching, two routes were taken to achieve such transformation: character training and family/community relationship. These hidden aspects of the traditional master-disciple relationship provide guidelines and impetus for the discovery of purpose and meaning.

CHAPTER 1

Perspective and Philosophy

Yin Fu style ba gua, as transmitted by fourth-generation lineage holder Gong Baozai, represents the highest standard of practice of the revered Eight Trigrams Boxing teaching. Gong Baozai described ba gua quan as embodying the essence of all forms and styles of *wu shu.*

The curriculum presented in the following pages is the system Gong Baozai (1904–2000) identified as that passed down to his teacher, third-generation lineage holder Gong Baotian (1871–1943), by second-generation lineage holder Yin Fu (1841–1911). It can only be speculated as to what first-generation lineage holder Dong Haichuan (1813–1882) transmitted to Yin Fu in the latter half of the nineteenth century. There has been much debate in the martial arts field about what comprised the original system. Disagreement as to the system's name—*ba gua quan,* "eight trigrams fist," versus *ba gua zhang,* "eight trigrams palm"—illustrates the level of discrepancy of understandings among practitioners. Gong Baozai asserted that ba gua quan was the actual "root" system possessed by Dong Haichuan, and that ba gua zhang is a significant, yet partial, dimension derived from the original work.

Evidence supporting the authenticity of Gong Baotian's ba gua quan is the historical fact that he was the third successor of an elite imperial security guard position in the Qing dynasty palace. Dong Haichuan, upon his retirement, had passed the post to Yin Fu; and Yin Fu, when he retired, had in turn handed it to Gong Baotian. The first-rate caliber of personal development and skill required to protect the royal family makes it highly probable that each of these teachers would have disclosed all of his secrets to his successor.

The ability of "light skill" or "flying art" (*qing gong*), which was known to have been possessed by Dong Haichuan, Yin Fu, and Gong Baotian, is no longer found in contemporary ba gua practice. In the system taught by Gong Baozai, the principles, methodology, and training all lead the practitioner in the direction of qing gong. Failure of present generations (including that of

Gong Baozai) to actualize this skill is due more likely to unsupportive modern-day social conditions than to insufficient knowledge or lack of methodology, given the depth of training Gong Baozai received from Gong Baotian. The last known bearer of the flying art in this lineage, Gong Baotian began teaching Gong Baozai, a village relative, when Gong Baozai was seven years of age. He continued to teach him with great thoroughness and care across a span of thirty years. (According to Gong Baozai, Gong Baotian's dedication to teaching him was partly due to Gong Baozai's family having been a main financial supporter of Gong Baotian's family.)

In addition to the apparently full transmission of knowledge that occurred between these lineage holders, two additional factors support the position that the ba gua quan presented here is the root system. First, there is the availability of all the physical forms, which are listed in Appendix 2. Second, and more vital, is the two-track procedure for study, "inner cultivation" (*nei xiu*) and "external training" (*wai lian*), which leads a practitioner to a state of mind and body that harmoniously blends knowledge and capability. This fulfills the highest objective of ba gua cultivation: becoming a complete, well-rounded human being.

The system Gong Baozai passed down is an offshoot of the early Chinese science of change, in which understanding of the various phases of human metaphysical transformation and growth guides the procedure of physical training. According to Chinese science, the cosmic force of opposition or duality comes into play at the time of the energetic formation of the kidneys. In ba gua quan, this stage is called "two appearances" (*liang yi*). The empty-hand form, the "Art of Two Appearances," is dedicated to this dualistic realm of self-inquiry (see Appendix 1). Even though comprehensive self-understanding can be gained with such yogic research into duality, the process would be incomplete if one stopped there.

The number 8 represents the fully formed human in the physical world. To reach the level of understanding associated with the number 8, one must first conduct the inquiries associated with the numbers 2 and 4 (see Appendix 1).

In this Chinese science of change, the constant interplay between polar opposites, as represented in the theory of yin yang, is the core dynamic of all existence. Intrinsic to physical reality, this dynamic is expressed in the binary progression 2, 4, 8, found in the *I Ching,* or *Book of Changes.* The ba gua quan system, as an embodiment of these sequential laws, accounts for every major metaphysical concept and principle in traditional Chinese thought. In the *I Ching,* the binary progression 2, 4, 8 is interpreted macrocosmically in terms of the sixty-four hexagrams. In ba gua quan, it is accounted for microcosmically in the challenge all individuals undertake to gain command of their biological constitution and freedom from negative social conditioning.

Thus the curriculum, based on the science of change, aims at attainment beyond mastery of the physical body alone. Effectiveness in the world is sought after, which transcends expertise in a singular craft such as fighting (warriorship) or healing (scholarship). It even surpasses the Chinese cultural ideal of "unified scholar-warrior achievement" (*wen wu shuang chuan*). Gong Baozai taught that above these respectable levels of accomplishment another plateau exists, namely saintly virtue and prophetic power. A person in this stage manifests extraordinary qualities not typically associated with life in the mundane world.

It is for this reason that Gong Baozai held the standard of sainthood or prophetic capability as the highest purpose and most noble level of attainment of the ba gua discipline. While the pragmatic concern remains that of actualizing martial and healing skills, the greater goal is mastering the art of change and applying it to the everyday challenges we face in our lives.

Unfortunately, orthodox standards as outlined in *Way of the Saint: The Missing Link Between Chinese Medicine, Mysticism, and Martial Arts* have diminished in recent decades. The classical master-disciple and lineage culture no longer fosters adequate development of personal mastery as attained by the revered masters of old. Even if we were to revive the original standard and began to wield our bodies and minds with this level of mastery, there is no guarantee that the old structures could support human expansion and growth in these modern times. For this to come about, ba gua, like any other martial art, must adapt to a rapidly changing world.

To transform martial arts into effective practice, as idealized in the legends of the old masters, while capable of handling modern challenges, both student and teacher must agree to assume more independent responsibility. With respect to this mutual responsibility, it is necessary to reconsider the value of the ancient custom of limiting successorship to one person. Since the time of Dong Haichuan, the ba gua system has traditionally been passed down to a single successor, called the "cloak and bowl descendent" (*yi bo chuan ren*), that sole individual to whom the master gives the entire system, including the final secrets.

In the future, several "cloak and bowl descendants" in each generation will guide students in the discovery of how to apply ba gua principles to all aspects of life. This should help the art to flourish once again. It will always be left to the individual practitioner to pave his or her own path. However, the curriculum offered in this book also serves as a tool and framework to empower the community.

Chapter 2

The Spirit of the Work

The spirit of the work rests on the recognition that ba gua quan, as a tool for human survival, provides the means to adapt and change. Change permeates the entire ba gua practice, since it is the central tenet in the inquiry of eight trigrams and sixty-four hexagrams, as documented in the *I Ching*. There is much more to this profound system than a sophisticated form of internal strength training and a series of intricate combat techniques based on eight palms.

Internal strength and combative skills, for all their benefits, are only one aspect of the human survival repertoire. If one's mental grasp of situations remains what Gong Baozai described as "following behind the horse's tail," one will always be a step behind, subject to the controlling forces of the world. An additional faculty is needed, where the mind and spirit develop the capacity to "lead in front of the horse's head." Thus one is able, in the manner of a commander, to capture the big picture of a situation. Then one can direct more capably the application of technique and strength. In ba gua quan, such ability is known as "before knowing, before feeling" (*xian zhi xian jue*).

The emphasis of most modern martial arts practice, as skewed toward physical feats of skill and strength, has reduced respect for a discipline whose masters were once revered for their completeness as well-rounded human beings. This matter is relevant today even to the pugilist who, for all his courage, power, and aggression, is as subject as anyone to the over-arching forces that threaten world existence.

By constantly testing the limits of the methods and principles of the traditional system, modern practitioners are encouraged to seek more effective ways to engage the ba gua quan inquiry. Increased active involvement in the progressive steps of one's personal transformation makes one a living contributor to the evolution of the system. In paving one's own path within the framework of the system, there is the opportunity—without rebellion or disrespect—for the practitioner to tap the system beyond the capabilities of one's teacher. Historically, representatives of one generation may not have aspired to, or attained, the highest ideal of the system. This limitation does not have to prevent future generations from realizing change along the broadest possible spectrum.

Master-disciple relationships, in the days of the martial-warrior hero, were based on fear and opposition. This was the agreement so that adequate pressure could be imposed upon a disciple to bring forth extraordinary achievement. The severe temperament of such a master was an expression of the spirit of one who had gone through exceedingly harsh self-restraint and discipline for the sake of harnessing survival abilities and deadly skills. In knowing the profound investment needed for such attainment, one might hesitate to relinquish this tried-and-true course of training out of concern that the standard would deteriorate. Without adequate marshalling of life forces, it would be difficult, especially at the beginning stages of training, to establish an imperturbable foundation.

Nonetheless, classical teaching methods, which often include manipulative withholding of approval or information until a chosen facet of character is changed, lie in discord with the modern consciousness that seeks to foster forthrightness and harmony in relationships.

In searching for a balancing element to competition as the means of achieving mastery in warriorship, another model was created. It was observed that the old "deficiency model," in which students are taught to identify primarily with what they do not know or have, relative to others, leaves the students feeling discontent, incomplete, and overly dependent on outside forces for fulfillment. Promotion of such an attitude alone only further contributes to the decay of global integrity, in that it does not foster a spirit of individual responsibility. Gong Baozai believed that today's declining standard could be reversed when "martial strength" is complemented by "martial principle." In the early days of orthodoxy, martial principle was the motivational and regulating force behind martial strength.

Reinstating martial principle to its original place of importance transforms the process into an "abundance model," which provides two things. It enables both teaching and learning to be conducted with a spirit of generosity, and it makes objective principle available as the universal reference point.

The clearer and more resilient one's inner principles, the greater, more lasting, and all-encompassing is one's strength. Benefits are clearly detailed in the curriculum such that the practitioner can responsibly pursue his or her goals.

Discipleship, teachership, and mastership represent three formal relationships with the world, upon which a fourth echelon, the Way of the Prophet or Saint, is placed. In honoring a final step toward fluidity, happiness, potential for love, and freedom, the Way of the Prophet or Saint refines the standard. A renewed spirit is fostered, whereby faith and hope presides over anger and fear.

The levels of attainment may be represented as follows:

- **Discipleship:** Foundation skills in scholarship and warriorship
- **Teachership:** Expertise gained in separate fields of scholarship (e.g. academics) and warriorship (e.g. athletics)
- **Mastership:** Unification of scholarship and warriorship
- **Way of the Prophet or Saint:** Unlimited changeability, formlessness

This structure, upon which the present curriculum is based, attempts to permit expression of the loftiest desires and expectations of modern practitioners within an ancient, formerly patriarchal system. The framework seeks to engender the achievement of two goals: mastery of the ancient system, and the healing of humanity.

Between the dual motives of self-fulfillment and service to others, tension is inevitably created. The new model makes active use of this tension by encouraging students to teach, beginning from the earliest ranks. Although social discord may arise from the readily observable limitations of a teacher who is not yet fully formed, perseverance provides the practitioner with the opportunity for complete fulfillment of both goals. This system proposes to make the highest level of attainment available to everyone.

CHAPTER 3

Developing Character

Gong Baozai stated that to become a "complete, well-rounded human being" is the single most important private accomplishment in life. Character training was a master's benevolent gesture, designed to help the disciple achieve this goal. Traditionally, character training took many forms. Behavior, core values, and beliefs were shaped through fine arts, calligraphy, the study of history and literature, and corrections to martial arts forms and applications. All contributed to smoothing the rough edges of one's personality and character. The highest ideal of orthodox martial arts is thus consistent with Yin Fu ba gua quan's central aim, which honors mental, emotional, physical, and energetic boundaries with other people.

In the past, the approaches to accomplishing this goal were oftentimes painful and severe. "Good character" was rated by the extent physical martial practice was mastered, as one remained loyal and obedient to the master's charge. Unquestioning adherence to the beliefs and values of one's culture was part of this means of ensuring social harmony.

The rules governing social harmony are different today. In this global-oriented, multiethnic world, there has been a breakdown of premodern traditional cultural patterns. There is thus the need to reevaluate basic approaches. In fostering this transition, the concept of character is foremost. The one-dimensional nature of old-style character deemed it fitting to pit one group against another. By contrast, modern-style character, while emphasizing adherence to customs and rules of society, allows for expression of the needs of individuals. Dual awareness, required to respect and honor the needs of another as oneself, constitutes a premier spiritual challenge of the modern age.

Friendship is a fundamental requisite of balanced character development. One can develop character as a scholar or a warrior, but that does not necessarily create a well-rounded human being. A vital component of principled leadership, friendship entails a loyalty based on truly caring for the welfare and happiness of another. Students can exhibit this loyalty by maintaining compassion if exposed to the teacher's failings, while not expecting an equal relationship. The teacher, in always placing the student's needs above his or her own, acts as a true friend to the student.

Guided by this new paradigm, and designed to accommodate a new individuality not bound to a single culture, learning begins by first using one's teacher as a primary relationship model. The dual-natured development of character starts with examining real-life exchanges between practitioner and instructor. In the learning environment, the instructor models, on all levels, appropriate boundaries and appropriate use of energy. While unfailing integrity is not expected until the highest ranks are achieved, students will inevitably observe and learn from what the instructor models.

In this safe environment, the practitioner has the opportunity to outwardly demonstrate character in relationship with teacher and classmates. In a group setting, such as a class, the ability of the student to monitor and be responsible for his or her behavior goes beyond the type of politeness that is customary in society. The practitioner begins to develop an awareness of the energetic support or drain that he or she can create when interacting with others.

In time, and with advancement into increasing responsibility as a teacher, the practitioner starts to incorporate into his or her training the teacher-to-student relationship dynamic. As a result, a new awareness of inner character starts to form that is an essential complement to the outer character being shaped by the physical practice. In this way, one learns the energetic responsibilities of leadership, and eventually of mastery.

Beginners, in general, are not expected to possess an in-depth model of useful, responsible behavior. This does not imply that no standard of behavior exists for students. Rather, it recognizes that for most, the standard of behavior aimed for in orthodox traditions is an extraordinary one. Whereas the typical sign of attainment in high-level practice is the ability to perform impeccable acts, this must in fact come second. Impeccability in one's intention to adhere to such traits as honesty, clarity, and forthrightness, as well as compassion, selflessness, and devotion in everything one does, must come first.

Chapter 4

Developing Proper Power

Of the many elements of character development, two are elusive and therefore most difficult. They are the proper acquisition and then use of power. In developing leadership of the caliber of great traditions, power must be pursued with integrity.

Two qualities stand out in a leader who seeks far-reaching benefit to humanity. These traits, in fact, define a leader's mastery. One is "spirit qi" (*shen qi*), personal attainment observable in one's carriage and posture, and in one's moral and social conduct. The other, "depth and profundity of learning" (*shen du*), is portrayed in one's compassionate sophistication in the ways of the world. The two are closely related.

Profundity of knowledge and skill is largely determined by the integrity with which power was procured. When proper deference and credit is given to all sources, power exchanges can be identified as either upright or lacking integrity.

Teacher and student may differ in their values. Thus, consideration is first given to traditional customs of respect and deference. The possibility that a traditional custom might be outdated can then be considered. Should such a departure be made, the alternative will be clearly spelled out and discussed by both parties. No residual air of rebellion or doubt concerning the source of the idea will be created. Priority having been given to principle, future discord is averted.

Principled self-mastery requires more than faith, sincerity, and talent. In order to prevent craftiness or self-deception, a complete system must provide the means to real clarity. The ability to effectively separate thought from feeling is the essence of clarity. The process is depicted in Chinese medicine as an opening from outside to inside.

Gong Baozai described four stages of character transformation:

Stage 1: Cultivation of "source qi" (*di qi*)

Stage 2: Opening of "energetic channels" (*jing mai*) and "tendon channels" (*jing jin*)

Stage 3: Training of the energetic and tendon channels in a way in which the influence penetrates directly into the "five organs and six bowels" (*wu zang liu fu*), that is, the internal organs

Stage 4: "Refinement of one's nature and temperament through rectification of character" (*gai zheng xing ge*)

The first three stages of transformation follow a systematic and predictable route. The fourth stage, refinement of nature and temperament, is often problematic. Jealousy, greed, fear, anger, and other desires must be adequately resolved with balanced development of the physical and energetic structures to be achieved. Leadership, when coming from a distorted structural base, will not effectively address the needs of the world.

Refinement of nature and temperament cannot be separated from expansion of intelligence. Expansion of intelligence cannot be separated from sculpting of the inner body. Sculpting of the inner body is required for attaining authentic skills. Creating a connection between moral conduct and extraordinary ability is a primary goal of ba gua practice.

In coveting only the external system, one may procure power but still lack the discrimination needed to appropriately wield it in complex human affairs. In coveting only human relationships, feelings and analytical processes tend to dominate. In both cases, the capacity for change is biased, and thus the individual does not achieve true freedom. *Without a moral reference point in the physical body to serve as a material basis for the moral conscience, one's purpose and mission may not match one's true needs or the needs of the world.*

A great persona, said Gong Baozai, can "break open below heaven" (*da kai tian xia*) toward the end of creating peaceful, revolutionary transformation in the world. This requires awareness of the difference between big effects and small effects. Adaptability as a leader must correspond with change in the world, and do so in a "socially proper and appropriate" (*zheng zheng dang dang*) fashion. Promoting clarity and resolution, rather than division and disunity, the masterful way is selfless.

Part II

The Curriculum

The orthodox ba gua quan system offers a framework that can be divided in four general categories: Discipleship, Teachership, Mastership, and Way of the Prophet or Saint. Each represents a stage in the evolutionary progression from a mind-body state that is attached to form to one free from form—the ideal state for role modeling and leadership. A ranking system embodying the above proceeds from Red Sash 1 to Black Sash 8. The various requirements in the Yin Fu ba gua quan curriculum are presented within four achievement classifications: forms, performance, scholarship, and instructor requirements.

CHAPTER 5

The Ranking System

Martial arts strives to achieve deadly fighting and extraordinary healing skills. However, in ba gua quan such skills do not emerge prematurely. Emphasis on "principle above strength" requires that only after significant character development has occurred, and by virtue of inner and outer attainment, does one earn the right to the higher secrets.

The ranking system was originated to provide clear-cut requirements for training and advancement. One of the challenges was to transform a complex, multidimensional, authority-based system into a clear, leadership-oriented curriculum of study. This was deemed necessary for the survival of the art. Both in terms of number of practitioners and standard of practice, success will depend on accommodating a new breed of practitioner. Three factors were considered in the design of the ranking system:

- the need to accommodate new generations of practitioners not familiar with classical Chinese language, custom, and culture
- the need to uphold the orthodox teaching standard in circumstances in which the highest-ranking teacher has not mastered the art to the highest degree
- the need to fully embrace the involvement of women, who today possess unprecedented opportunities for leadership and responsibility

By modernizing hierarchical methods of character training to honor student independence and equality, a growing population of teachers will be accommodated. Teachers who follow this program, at their early stages of development, will not likely possess the discrimination to render impeccable discipline onto others. To assist them during this critical phase, the ranking system has designed into it a framework that fosters the automatic self-transformation of character. This is in acknowledgement that character is a critical facet to a teacher's effectiveness in advancing others in knowledge and skill. Rather than confrontation, the system promotes mutual expansion and benefit, and thus fosters a long-term student-teacher relationship.

Gong Baotian often reminded Gong Baozai that "there is no number one under heaven" and that "if one does not exercise discrimination when sharing with others, it is impossible to grow." Well-rounded development, as reflected in the ranking system, entails consciously shifting the emphasis away from selfish ambition to commitment to the entire community.

The Ba Gua Quan Ranking System Charts

Descriptions of the required capabilities for advancement, as detailed in the ranking system charts on the following pages, will enable students to set individually chosen, concrete goals, pursued at their own pace. Explanations of each rank and specific characteristics of the skills to be learned and mastered will provide a clear course of study so that student-teacher interactions can be straightforward, positive, and comprised of clear, cooperative objectives.

Four categories of attainment, covering the progression of development, are delineated by the titles of *Disciple, Teacher, Master,* and *Prophet* or *Saint.* Each is represented by a colored or black sash, with varying numbers of stripes. The accompanying qualities, "following," "leading," "teaching," and "being/role-modeling," depict the types of relationship skills needed to enact one's goals. The breadth of this framework provides even advanced practitioners with space to grow. Ranks are no longer, as in old times, given on the basis of inherited position or entitlement, but are required to be earned, in part, through active role modeling in community leadership.

Implicit in the curriculum of the ranking system are two tracks: one for men and one for women. These two tracks within ba gua quan training have been developed to honor differences in female and male conditioning, character, and constitution. Traditionally, men and women, at least for a period of intensive study and research, trained separately. A teacher's experience with men's and women's training will determine the extent to which the two methodologies are implemented.

Discipleship – Following

Sash	Required Capabilities
Red 1	**Forms:** Eight Standing Meditations
Red 2	**Forms:** Root Stances • 4 Inner Mother Palms • Pao Chui Lines 1–4 • Simple Single Palm Change • Pushing Palm
Red 3	**Forms:** 4 Outer Mother Palms • Pao Chui Lines 5–8 • Lower Piercing Palm • Changing Palm in Four Postures • Plum Flower Post Training

Teachership – Leadership

Sash	Title	Required Capabilities
Black 1	Junior Instructor	**Forms:** Eight Mother Palms (Ba Mu Zhang) • San Shou Fixed Step • Oblique Palm **Performance:** 4 fixed applications (3X each side) • Beginning sparring **Scholarship:** Pao Chui Map **Instructor Requirements:** Fitness • Yoga, Pilates, or other mind-body training
Black 2	Associate Instructor	**Forms:** Two Appearances Fist • San Shou Moving Steps • 1st Palace Fist **Performance:** 8 fixed applications (3X each side) **Instructor Requirements:** 1 year weekly instructing; min. 100 hours instructing • Character diary
Black 3	Instructor	**Forms:** Four Images Fist • Form 1 of 2-Person Set **Performance:** Artful Sparring • 16 fixed applications (3X each side) **Instructor Requirements:** 2 years weekly instructing; min. 100 hours / year • 1st Weapons Form
Black 4	Senior Instructor (Lao shi)	**Forms:** Eight Palm Fist • Empty Hand vs. Broadsword—Weapons • 2nd, 3rd Palace Fist • 3rd Weapons Form **Performance:** Artful sparring • 16 Multiple fixed applications • Control over physical fitness **Instructor Requirements:** Create own class; min. 3 continuing students for 2 years • min. 200 hours / year; min. 2 classes / week • Graduate student to Black 1

Mastership – Teaching Teachers

Sash	Title	Required Capabilities
Black 5	Junior Master	**Forms:** Form 2 of 2-Person Set • 4th Weapons Form • Advanced San Shou techniques • 8 Palms Fist Walks into 8 Mother Palms • 4th, 5th Palace Fist **Performance:** Freestyle vs. 1 opponent • Chains of application, one after another **Instructor Requirements:** Begin study of another system
Black 6	Master (Shi fu, Shi mu)	**Forms:** Yin Yang Palms • Ten Step Fist • 5th Weapons Form • All pipeline forms **Performance:** Ling Shou • Freestyle vs. 2 opponents • Separate Qi from Strength **Scholarship:** Write scholar-warrior thesis **Instructor Requirements:** Graduate student to Black 3

Way of the Prophet or Saint – Being / Role Modeling

Sash	Title	Required Capabilities
Black 7	Senior Master	**Performance:** Freestyle vs. 4 opponents **Scholarship:** Eight Palm Methods **Instructor Requirements:** Graduate student to Black 5; Achieve black belt/sash in another system
Black 8	Grand Master (Da shi)	**Performance:** Freestyle vs. 8 opponents **Scholarship:** Latter steps of ba gua meditation **Instructor Requirements:** Graduate student to Black 7 • Develop new applications • Create an independent original work or act whose goal is service to all humanity

Notes

- Capability includes proper physical execution appropriate to the rank and recitation of proper names for each movement.
- Every level includes the requirements of all previous levels.
- For all ranks Junior Master and above, classes must be maintained with a minimum of three continuing students.
- The "learning by teaching policy" allows Junior Instructors and above to instruct students unsupervised, in all forms and exercises certified for that rank.

CHAPTER 6

Understanding Discipleship

"One year minor endeavor, three years major results."

Following is an in-depth description of the required curriculum for ranks Red 1, Red 2, and Red 3, comprising the discipleship phase of training.

RED 1

Depicted in the list of ba gua quan system forms in Appendix 2 are two tracks of learning, one internal and one external.

Conceptual difficulties at the beginning phase of learning are common. The student may ask, "What does it mean to be doing an exercise externally or internally?" This single question permeates the entire study at every level of inquiry.

Study thus commences with a simple yet profound internal-external integration exercise called Eight Standing Meditations. This routine, inspired by insights Gong Baozai had into the development of balanced skill, and by women's research in the United States, gives the beginner an immediate experience of the unification of the body's internal and external forces.

Before one can expect to recognize the principles of correct posture while in movement, one must experience correct posture in stillness. Before one can grasp the mystery of circular strength, one must know its linear circuitry. The particular brand of strength sought after in ba gua is natural and effortless, generated out of proper alignment of structure, rather than willfully, through use of strenuous effort.

Curriculum

- **Eight Standing Meditations** (*zhan ba mu zhang*) – a series of eight stationary palm postures, divided into four inner palms and four outer palms. The eight separate body organs or regions represent the core of the eight trigrams inquiry.
  Characteristics: Practiced in stillness; high shallow stance, cultivates "reed breathing"; emphasizes fostering awareness of the physical

structure and balance rather than on the development of *qi* or strength; awareness developed of the eight cardinal directions—above, below, inside, outside, back, front, left, and right.

RED 2

The student is introduced to participation in an authentic martial art lineage. Exercises from the system open the skeletal, muscular, and fascia structures of the body. One begins to get in touch with one's health status relative to the demands of the training. Introduced are Eight Mother Palms (*ba mu zhang*), the circular mother form of the Yin Fu ba gua system; Cannon Fist (*pao chui*), the linear father form of the system; as well as Single Changing Palm (*dan huan zhang*), the preliminary circle-walking posture.

Curriculum

- **Root Stances –** horse riding posture, bow and arrow stance, and containing opportunities stance (*han ji bu*).
  Characteristics: develops open, flexible body; awareness of outer character; coordination among the "three outer correspondences" (*san wai he*): shoulder-hip, elbow-knee, hand-foot.
- **Four Inner Mother Palms –** palm postures that represent heart, lung, liver, and kidney organs.
  Characteristics: drives the qi inward toward the internal organs, opens fascia connection between limbs and internal organs.
- **Pao Chui Lines 1–4 –** the first 32 movements of the 64-movement sequence (see Appendix 4).
  Characteristics: exercises memory; emphasizes flexibility and quickness of the body and the execution of a wide variety of techniques; develops endurance and power.
- **Simple Single Palm Change –** rudimentary method used to change directions in circle walking, with the Single Changing Palm.
  Characteristics: teaches smooth transition between left and right, right and left.
- **Pushing Palm (Single Changing Palm) –** the cardinal position held when practicing circle walking.
  Characteristics: emphasizes mud-stepping footwork (*tang ni bu*) in the training of long breathing, endurance, and strength.

Red 3

The student has already demonstrated commitment to the foundation work and is now seeking inspiration as well as concrete criteria for training and for evaluating his or her advancement.

The concept of the highest standard of character—to honor oneself and others—illustrates to the beginner that movements on the physical level need to be harmonious with movement within one's own body, as well as with what is presented by the outside world. In this way, the philosophy begins to guide one's actions; standards governing character and the physical begin to meet.

The relationship theme of the Art of Discipleship is "following." The student begins to be aware of proper and improper relationship behaviors for obtaining power. The association between character development and physical ability begins to be learned.

Working through emotional resistance can bring one unprecedented breakthrough. When, as a result, movements can be learned faster, it signifies the beginnings of one's discovery of the relationship between martial arts, Chinese medicine, and nonphysical levels of being.

Curriculum

- **Four Outer Mother Palms –** palm postures that represent head, back, waist, and abdomen regions.
  Characteristics: drives the qi outward to the outer body regions, opens fascia connections between the limbs and the muscles via the internal organs.
- **Pao Chui Lines 5–8 –** the last 32 movements of the 64-movement sequence (see Appendix 4).
  Characteristics: exercises memory; emphasizes flexibility and dexterity of the body, and the execution of a wide variety of techniques; develops endurance and power.
- **Lower Piercing Palm –** a fundamental transition move in Eight Mother Palms.
  Characteristics: promotes flexibility in the legs and waist.
- **Changing Palm in Four Postures (*huan zhang si shi*) –** a series of four basic movements, plus one extra, which is essential to safe Eight Mother

Palms practice (see Appendix 9). As training improves in Eight Mother Palms practice, postures can shunt more qi and blood to the target organs. Then it is necessary to be mindful during the transitions between the palm postures, as well as when switching sides using the same posture. Qi and blood must be given a chance to leave the organ or body region where it had accumulated, and redistribute harmoniously through the rest of the body.

Characteristics: performed rhythmically and smoothly in coordination with breathing and with full engagement of conscious intent. The key is to maintain balanced structural correspondence among body parts, ensuring that qi and blood are flowing evenly, from one posture to the next.

- **Plum Flower Post Training –** the three basic root stances are performed in alternating patterns atop five posts.
  Characteristics: traditionally practiced on wooden posts planted in the ground, or uses wooden blocks or bricks as substitute.

CHAPTER 7

Understanding Teachership

"To know what one knows, and know what one does not know; that's to know."

Following is an in-depth description of the required curriculum for ranks Black 1, Black 2, Black 3, and Black 4, comprising the teachership phase of training.

JUNIOR INSTRUCTOR – BLACK 1

By the Junior Instructor level, the student has demonstrated sufficient commitment to begin growing through the system. Following the "learning by teaching policy," this is the first level whereby individuals may begin formally teaching their own students, independent of supervision. They are permitted to teach all forms that they have received certification for, as defined by their rank.

It is recognized how hard the student has worked to earn Black 1. The student is starting to show significant progress; this is expressed by the ability to demonstrate sufficient honor and control of his or her own forces, as well as the forces of another. Therefore, through physical contact with partners, elementary sparring and energetic work begins at this stage.

Curriculum

- **Ba Mu Zhang –** Eight Mother Palms, the Single Changing Palm, and the entire eight basic palm postures performed in one continuous flow around a six- to eight-foot-diameter circle (see Appendixes 6–8). The transition movements—Lower Piercing Palm, Changing Palm in Four Postures, and Oblique Palm—are employed interchangeably. *Characteristics:* can be performed as a 20- to 40-minute form; opens all the fascia connections and correspondences among the limbs, internal organs, and outer body regions.
- **San Shou Fixed Step –** rudimentary fixed sparring sequence, done while alternating between the basic forward arrow and backward sitting (*han ji bu*) stances.

Characteristics: introduction to Yin Fu ba gua elementary blocking and striking patterns; a means to strengthen and toughen the hands, arms, legs, and feet. Strengthens the stance, teaches one to resist oncoming multidirectional force.

- **Oblique Palm –** an advanced circle-walking transition maneuver
Characteristics: focuses on stretching the lateral aspect of the body.
- **Four fixed applications, three times each side –** rehearsed two-person applications demonstrating basic command of proper technique and strength against an opponent. Proficiency is marked by the ability to expertly perform techniques three times in rapid succession, on both left and right sides. Embodied within each application are specific root skills, such as timing, leveraging, and distance, which are essential components of "pure technique." They continue to be developed in freestyle application beginning at the Junior Master rank.
Characteristics: requires execution of "pure technique" with employment of a firm stance through proper positioning of legs, waist, and torso.
- **Beginning sparring –** slow, extremely light freeform sparring, with no contact made in the strikes; limited grabbing and throwing.
Characteristics: introduction to the experience of empty hand person-to-person confrontation; an opportunity to learn the basic ground rules of self-protection: positioning, distancing, balance, timing, footwork; begins an inquiry into simulated conflict and competition.
- **Pao Chui Map –** (see Appendix 3) the entire 64 movements are performed in one continuous flow within the ba gua diagram map.
Characteristics: enters at least once into each of all nine palaces: *kan, gen, zhen, shun, li, kun, dui, chien,* and the central axis.
- **Demonstration of basic fitness –** prearranged calisthenic routine.
Characteristics: group format: strength, endurance, and basic flexibility. Criterion is adjusted to student's health picture coming into training.
- **Yoga, Pilates, or other mind-body training –** highly recommended; helps one get in touch with structural mechanics, the body's core musculature, and the origins of physical movement.

Associate Instructor – Black 2

The Associate Instructor level of teaching incorporates a new requirement for consistency, as demonstrated by the ability to maintain an independent class that meets weekly for a minimum of one year. One begins to learn the skills and character necessary to establish loyal and productive relationships.

At this level of training, two tracks may emerge, honoring the unique strengths of women and men. Research has revealed differences between women and men. Men demonstrate greater ease and comfort in rigorous contact training and in sustaining the external structure of a community. Women exhibit greater ease and comfort in character development and in the tending of the spiritual welfare of the community.

Curriculum

- **Two Appearances Fist (*liang yi zhi shu*) –** designed to cultivate the body's qi; inquiry into the dual aspects of the self.
  Characteristics: performed softly, evenly, and smoothly; emphasizes flexibility and extension with the aim of passively "using qi to encourage strength."
- **San Shou Moving Steps –** moving steps are added to the San Shou Fixed Step.
  Characteristics: requires mobility and use of whole-body reflexes and strength.
- **First Palace Fist –** first of five known Palace Fists (Gong Baozai passed down only five of the total eight Palace Fists). Selection of the Palace Fist to be taught first is to be determined by the instructor, based on the individual student's need.
  Characteristics: each Palace Fist is devoted to movements and fighting applications derived from one particular organ or body region that is associated with one of the eight trigrams.
- **Eight fixed applications, three times each side –** the addition of four fixed applications.
  Characteristics: see "Four fixed applications" in Junior Instructor section.
- **One year instructing weekly with a minimum of 100 hours instructing –** this begins the process of developing long-term relationships and

the beginning of what may be learned in a position of leadership; brings to light hidden areas of delusion.
Characteristics: requires dedication, regularity, perseverance, discrimination, and integrity.

- **Compiling a Personal Character Diary –** see Appendix 12.
Characteristics: utilizes a personal journal, notes, written assignments, and formal writings handed down from one's teacher on the teaching and learning experience and the system.

Instructor – Black 3

By the time one becomes an instructor, an exclusive commitment is clear. Having already taught for a minimum of two years, this investment is on the level of a part-time profession. At this stage, proper attention is given to an appropriate energy exchange in the form of monetary payments from student to teacher.

Monetary exchange becomes a topic of voluntary study rather than merely a binding obligation. This is designed to facilitate the flow of recognition and energy between lower generations and upper generations through the instructor. Therefore, these payments reflect not only the agreement between student and teacher, but an awareness of the heart and energy investment that has been made by the teacher's own instructor. This agreement maintains the proper spirit for the character of the student and the teacher in a way that moves the work properly forward.

Curriculum

- **Four Images Fist (*si xiang quan*) –** designed to develop the body's strength; inquiry into the four aspects of the self.
Characteristics: performed evenly and smoothly but with particular emphasis on hardness and strength; aims to actively "use strength to propel the qi."
- **Form One of Two-Person Set –** prearranged sparring set of the Lohan tradition.
Characteristics: develops intricacy of hand- and footwork, as well as the spirit of orthodox martial combat.
- **Artful Sparring –** conscious employment of proper attitude, posture, and techniques representative of the Yin Fu ba gua style of fighting.

Characteristics: requires self-control, discipline, awareness, and ability to focus inwardly on self-regulation while engaging external forces.

- **Sixteen fixed applications, three times each side –** the addition of eight fixed applications.
  Characteristics: see "Eight fixed applications" in Associate Instructor section.
- **Two years of continuous weekly instructing with a minimum of 100 hours instructing per year –** this continues the process of developing long-term relationships and what may be learned in a position of leadership; brings to light hidden areas of delusion.
  Characteristics: requires dedication, regularity, perseverance, and integrity. Additionally, the instructor must inculcate a feeling of trust, loyalty, and motivation in the students.
- **First Weapons Form –** one of the four classical Chinese martial art weapons: broadsword (*dao*), double-edge sword (*jian*), spear (*qiang*), and staff (*gun*).
  Characteristics: selection is determined by the instructor and tailored to the individual student.

Senior Instructor – Black 4

A Senior Instructor has demonstrated sufficient command of the system to be considered a representative at a level entitled to the honorific *Lao Shi,* "Honorable Teacher." At this level, the required capabilities begin to embody more than physical training and basic teaching. A beginning awareness emerges of the ba gua quan system as an integrated process of mind, body, and spirit development. This is exemplified by the requirement for control over one's physical fitness and for maintaining sufficiently productive relationships of such an enduring nature so as to be able to lead a student to the attainment of the rank of Junior Instructor (Black 1).

Adequate expertise is demonstrated through the command of not only the performance of the physical forms, but also in the ability to exhibit sufficient command of the principles behind the forms, so that sparring is done in an artful manner. Proper posture is adhered to, leading to techniques that are applied in a thoughtful way. One has gained sufficient proficiency so as to neither compromise one's own physical integrity nor that of an opponent.

Curriculum

- **Eight Palm Fist –** based on the eight separate mother palms rendered into a linear form (Appendix 10), specifically for teaching fighting applications of the eight palm techniques.
  Characteristics: requires aggressive movement, precision, mental alertness; requires an ability to quickly differentiate one palm disposition from another.
- **Second Weapons Form: Empty Hand vs. Broadsword –** the second of the weapons forms: empty hand versus a weapon-wielding opponent.
  Characteristics: is athletic, develops acute vision, timing, distance, speed, and correct emphasis of strength.
- **Second Palace Fist –** second of five known Palace Fists of the original eight Palace Fists; selection of to be determined by the instructor and tailored to the individual student.
  Characteristics: each Palace Fist is devoted to movements and fighting applications derived from one particular organ or body region that is associated with one of the eight trigrams.
- **Third Palace Fist –** see "Second Palace Fist," above.
- **Third Weapons Form –** see "First Weapons Form" in Instructor section.
  Characteristics: selection is determined by the instructor and tailored to the individual student.
- **Artful Sparring –** conscious employment of proper attitude, posture, and techniques representative of the Yin Fu ba gua style of fighting.
  Characteristics: requires self-control, discipline, awareness, and ability to focus inwardly on self-regulation while engaging external forces.
- **Sixteen multiple fixed applications –** of the sixteen fixed applications learned for the Instructor rank, for each application one change must be demonstrated, thereby creating a chain of two linked applications that are connected by principle.
  Characteristics: develops foresight, anticipation, and the beginnings of a scientific perspective of combat based upon the principle of change.
- **Control over physical fitness –** has developed and maintained a daily personal practice that promotes overall health, flexibility, strength, and endurance, sufficient to enable the practitioner to endure the rigors of advanced training. This should be concretely reflected in the beginnings

of balance and health in one's real-life relationships, as assessed by subjective/objective evaluation of the examiners, through interview, and by review of the practitioner's diary.
Characteristics: is signified by body weight and shape, strength and flexibility, vigor, and mental clarity appropriate to one's constitution and history. Externally, is signified by the beginnings of well-rounded professional, social, and family life lived in accord with one's mission of service.

- **Creates a class with a minimum of three continuing students over two years of study, with a minimum of 200 hours of instructions per year, and a minimum of two classes per week –** the highest level of Teachership before the Mastership level begins.
  Characteristics: is a seasoned instructor who has experienced many of the challenges and rewards of leadership and who has persevered both in her personal studies as well as in his or her service to the system. Is indicated by the culmination of leadership skills, physical training, and character development, proven by the respect shown by his or her students, peers, and instructors in the community; entitles the practitioner to the honorific *lao shi.*
- **Graduate a student to Black 1 (Junior Instructor) –** the first formal demonstration of teaching skill and effective leadership.
  Characteristics: as a Senior Instructor, demonstrates the ability to maintain a relationship with a student, sufficient to train the student to the level of achievement required for Junior Instructor.

CHAPTER 8

Understanding Mastership

"More than control of behavior is needed to transform the temperament; faith, honesty, and sincerity cannot be manufactured externally."

Following is an in-depth description of the required curriculum for ranks Black 5 and Black 6, comprising the mastership phase of training.

JUNIOR MASTER – BLACK 5

Potentials for mastery have begun to emerge. The Junior Master can see things and maybe see an appropriate course of action, but cannot yet, by his or her own dircction, develop an efficient plan and enact it on another's behalf.

The intensity of study increases dramatically, continuing at a Master level. Many new forms are added to the curriculum, signifying the student's increased capacity for assimilation in both mental and physical realms. Therefore, the most significant characteristic of engagement, on the Junior Master level, is the increased time and energy required for self-development.

At this stage of mastery, maintaining self-integrity while sparring is not enough. Nor is it sufficient to combatively beat an opponent. Familiarity with the external expressions of strength of the eight palm postures, as learned through the fixed applications up to the Senior Instructor rank, is needed. The Junior Master begins to spontaneously apply techniques that are in accordance with inner and outer principles. "Principle above strength" is the automatic response to an unpredictable attack by an opponent.

Maintenance of healthy relationships with students and teachers remains an essential component of this level. However, emphasis returns to inward exploration. The Junior Master is no longer concerned with learning physical abilities alone, but is now dedicated to self-reflection, the evaluation of conditioned beliefs, and such questions as "What do we mean by principle?" and "How does this action I am now performing agree or disagree with principle?" Such an inquiry is necessary preparation for the emerging Master level activity of bringing lessons discovered inwardly fully into existence in the material world.

Curriculum

- **Form Two of Two-Person Set –** second of two prearranged sparring sets of the Lohan tradition.
  Characteristics: maintains sense of the four cardinal directions while engaged with an opponent; uses increased hand and foot combinations.
- **Fourth Weapons Form –** at instructor's discretion; see "First Weapons Form" in Instructor section.
- **Advanced San Shou techniques –** added to the basic "three hands" (*san shou*) sequence performed with fixed and live steps, are additional "four hands" (*si shou*), "five hands" (*wu shou*), "six hands" (*liu shou*), "seven hands" (*qi shou*), and so on, prearranged sequences.
  Characteristics: performs this evenly and slowly at first, then eventually with full speed and power; learns these short application-sequences designed to teach strategic combinations, with an emphasis on learning to instinctively flow with the direction of movement.
- **Eight Palms Fist Walks into Eight Mother Palms –** the linear Eight Palms Fist form is dissected and incorporated into the Eight Mother Palms circle-walking routine.
  Characteristics: challenges the depth of comprehension of the two forms; requires research into the deeper significance of individual movements; discovers ways to link separate movements together in a manner that adheres to the Three Essential Standards: principle of structure, principle of medicine, and principle of technique.
- **Fourth Palace Fist –** see "Second Palace Fist" in Senior Instructor section.
- **Fifth Palace Fist –** see "Second Palace Fist" in Senior Instructor section.
- **Freestyle sparring versus one opponent –** ability to execute "perfect technique" in freestyle sparring situation against a single opponent.
  Characteristics: requires ability to draw out internal strength in techniques in the language of the Yin Fu ba gua system.
- **Chains of applications, one after another –** an exercise that bridges the fixed applications and freestyle fighting; applications are performed as a chain in semi-prearranged fashion.
  Characteristics: demonstrates concentration on the logic of change.
- **Begin study of another traditional mind-body discipline**
  Characteristics: does not have to be martial arts; broadens a student's

experiential horizons; discerns the strengths and limits of the Yin Fu ba gua tradition in all its respects.

Master – Black 6

A Master has demonstrated sufficient command of the system to be considered a representative at a level entitled to the honorific *shi fu* or *shi mu* ("teacher-father" or "teacher-mother"). One who has achieved this rank has mastered all the forms comprising the curriculum of the Yin Fu ba gua quan system. This is exemplified by meeting the requirement for maintaining sufficiently productive relationships of such an enduring nature as to be able to lead a student to the attainment of the rank of Instructor (Black 3).

In addition to exemplifying healthy relationships with students, teachers, and peers, a Master is able to effectively demonstrate the principles of the system in discourse with people outside the martial arts community.

The attainment of mastership signifies that one has a grasp of the traditional martial art system, in its myriad complexities. Looking back at what has been attained, the Master recognizes that the process by which the transformation has taken place was a "mysterious transmission" (*xuan chuan*) from his or her Master. A grasp of increasingly finer subtleties and feelings are paramount in the experience of one who has achieved this level of personal development. To the extent the Master is known by the public, he or she is recognized as an undeniably extraordinary individual, in honesty and integrity, as well as in knowledge and capability.

Arising from full embodiment of the heart and soul of a teacher-father or teacher-mother, the compassionate desire to further the enlightenment of others leads to selfless and effortless service. Through such unending dedication, a Master of this system earns the right to access the deepest mysteries in the technical craft of hand-to-hand fighting hidden within the system. This enables him or her to conduct an inquiry on more than physical, emotional, and mental levels. A Master has the ability, based on the possession of strength and power, to steadfastly persevere in the face of temptation in order to maintain impeccable conduct.

Curriculum

- **Yin Yang Palms –** a premier fighting form of the system; contains combinations of techniques drawn from the eight palms.

Characteristics: emphasizes especially knowing the yin and yang aspects of movements, as stated in the ba gua quan poem: "Yin yang hands turning above and below; sink the shoulders down to the elbows, returning qi to the *dan tian*."

- **Ten Step Fist** (*shi bu quan*) – Gong Baotian transmitted this form to Gong Baozai late in their relationship, advising him that mastery of this particular form would enable a practitioner to "protect one's life."
  Characteristics: masters ten essential leg maneuvers of the Yin Fu ba gua system; may be taught at earlier ranks based on teacher discretion.
- **Fifth Weapons Form (if not accomplished at Junior Master level) –** see "First Weapons Form" in Instructor section.
- **All Pipeline Forms –** Master-level proficiency in Cannon Fist, the Art of Two Appearances, Four Images Fist, Eight Palm Fist, Eight Mother Palms, and Eight Palm Fist Walking into Eight Mother Palms.
  Characteristics: memorizes names; shows ability to move target organs and body regions and to generate strength with movements; knows fighting applications of all techniques; gains intellectual knowledge of the 2 x 4 x 8 x 64 philosophy of Change; understands the pipeline forms in relation to the Traditional Chinese Origins of the Universe Theory (see Appendix 1), which is a template for the metaphysical development of the human being.
- **Ling Shou, various techniques –** a series of strategies and applications, many involving nongrappling ground maneuvers, with "scissors legs" (*jian cha tui*) as the central focus.
  Characteristics: requires quickness, agility, strength, balance, and flexibility.
- **Freestyle sparring versus two opponents –** ability to execute "perfect technique" in freestyle sparring versus two opponents.
  Characteristics: requires ability to draw out internal strength in techniques, in the language of Three Essential Standards and the Eight Mother Palms of the Yin Fu ba gua system.
- **Separate Qi from Strength –** the ability to demonstrate separation of either qi or strength in free movement; to be able to spontaneously manifest whichever emphasis is appropriate for any particular form, posture, or movement.

Characteristics: requires conceptual and yogic understanding of the distinction between Single Changing Palm and Double Changing Palm.

- **Write scholar-warrior thesis –** a minimum of one publication-quality article or report on some aspect of Yin Fu ba gua quan.
  Characteristics: writes (typically) in collaboration with or under the guidance of one's teacher; may use article(s) in preparation for the independent original work or act required for the rank of Grand Master.
- **Graduate a student to Black 3 (Instructor) –** this is the second formal demonstration of teaching skill and effective leadership.
  Characteristics: demonstrates, as a Master, the ability to maintain a relationship with a student sufficient to train the student to the level of achievement required for advancement to the rank of Instructor.

CHAPTER 9

Understanding the Way of the Prophet or Saint

"When the personality is too forceful or the temper too bad, the spirit is not light; elusive will be one's grasp of the subtle and mysterious."

Following is an in-depth description of the required curriculum for ranks Black 7 and Black 8, comprising the Way of the Prophet or Saint phase of training.

SENIOR MASTER – BLACK 7

Mastery of the physical forms of the curriculum has already been achieved at the Master *Shi Fu* / *Shu Mu* rank. At the Senior Master rank, there are no new forms introduced into the curriculum. At this level, the practitioner is engaging in increasingly complex research on how to manipulate her energies to deal with the world in increasingly fluid and formless ways. The system has been integrated into the practitioner, and she begins this advanced research by tapping the inspirational resources of the Way of the Prophet or Saint. As such, the basic ba gua goals of "even, balanced, open, and fluid" are expressed at unprecedented levels of awareness. This is exemplified by having maintained sufficiently productive relationships of such an enduring and intimate nature so as to be able to lead a student to the attainment of the rank of Junior Master (Black 5).

For those who enter study with a preexisting desire to serve humanity, the stages of learning, beginning in Red 1, represent the graded steps one can take to fulfill that dream. To ensure that the vision she holds is brought to fruition, to the fullest extent of her destiny and capability, completeness presupposes two things: (1) that the vision the practitioner holds is aligned with the greater world and (2) that the strategic course of study, from Red 1 to Black 8, can effectively transform the mind, body, soul, spirit, and character of the individual to prepare her to accomplish her vision of service.

Such a thorough inquiry is needed to weed out any residual delusions of personality, identity, and behavior, which in spite of the accomplishment of formidable knowledge and skills, would still render one unable to succeed in the task of leadership at the highest level. Of highest importance is the bringing forth of certain essential capabilities: (1) an accurate feeling for the truth of what is correct, (2) the power to generate momentum on one's own and to be the authentic spark for one's mission, and (3) the ability to handle all potentially disruptive forces that an adept, who carries the vision of a prophet or saint, shall inevitably encounter.

Curriculum

- **Freestyle Sparring versus four opponents –** ability to execute "perfect technique" in a freestyle sparring situation against four opponents.
  Characteristics: requires ability to draw out internal strength in techniques, in the language of the Eight Mother Palms of the Yin Fu ba gua system.
- **Eight Palm Methods –** eight basic ideas of strength representing an alternative treatment of Eight Mother Palms.
  Characteristics: requires complete personal embodiment of the Eight Trigrams principle in one's thoughts, feelings, and actions.
- **Graduate a student to Black 5 (Junior Master) –** this is the third formal demonstration of teaching skill and effective leadership.
  Characteristics: demonstrates, as Senior Master, the ability to maintain a relationship with a student sufficient to train them to the level of achievement required for Junior Master.
- **Achieve black belt/sash in another traditional mind-body discipline** – attains a rank equivalent to the level of a Junior Instructor (Black 1) in another discipline.
  Characteristics: does not have to be martial arts; broadens a student's experiential horizons; discerns the strengths and limits of the Yin Fu ba gua tradition in all its respects.

Grand Master – Black 8

A Grand Master has demonstrated sufficient command of the system to be considered a representative at a level entitled to the highest honorific *da shi* ("grand master"). One has become a living role model of all ethical and skill-related ideals of the standard and remains uncompromised by elements such as fashion, common desires, and political climate—that is, "fame and fortune" (*ming li*). This is also exemplified by having maintained sufficiently productive relationships, of the most enduring and intimate nature, to lead a student to the attainment of the rank of Senior Master (Black 7).

At this highest level of Mastership, not only has one gained a command of the objective art form, but also a comparable command of one's personal life, as well as of one's ability to bring forth, publicly, one's higher mission of service. Such attainment represents the highest expression of "inner and outer unity" (*nei wai he yi*). Gong Baozai called this the Way of the Prophet or Saint.

The Grand Master is awarded two sashes: a black sash with eight red stripes, and a gold sash with eight black stripes. The black sash is for use in training; the gold sash is used for ceremonial activities.

The physical tasks, outlined in the curriculum, were completed for the practitioner to be awarded the rank of Master. An added degree of formlessness was attained to earn the rank of Senior Master.

At the Grand Master stage, endeavors of world service become the preeminent activity. The practitioner regularly seeks to independently create original works and acts aimed at service to all humanity. In having transcended the boundaries of his or her physical form, the Grand Master is qualified as a standard bearer of the tradition. He or she is able to effectively engage in collaboration with individuals of other cultures, systems, and languages.

Attainment of the rank of Grand Master allows for sharing among equals of this rank. In promoting the spirit and practice of the system to such an extent, the Grand Master has become free from further obligation to his or her own master. This is the ultimate payback for both practitioner and teacher, whereby in selfless service to humanity, both his or her master and the system are honored with a higher form of payment than money, which until now has been the medium of energetic exchange.

Curriculum

- **Freestyle sparring versus eight opponents –** the ability to fluidly employ the Eight Palm Methods in defense and attack against eight opponents simultaneously symbolizes the highest attainment in Yin Fu ba gua quan and represents unlimited changeability using all possible changes.

Characteristics: demonstrates no-mind, one-effort, and continuous change.

- **Latter steps of ba gua meditation –** depending upon the teacher's discretion, latter steps meditation may be practiced at earlier ranks. The method is presented here, at the highest rank, to signify the unlimited potential of this procedure.
  Characteristics: utilizes intentional visual imagery with command over physical existence.
- **Graduate a student to Black 7 (Senior Master) –** this is the fourth and final formal demonstration of teaching skill and effective leadership.
  Characteristics: demonstrates, as a Grand Master, the ability to maintain a relationship with a student sufficient to train the student to the level of achievement required for Senior Master.
- **Develop new applications** – a formalized set of methods and techniques is contributed to the field.
  Characteristics: innovates from one's personal life experience, fighting style, and specialized training.
- **Create an independent original work or act whose goal is service to all humanity –** represents the highest attainment possible through this system.
  Characteristics: having transcended the boundaries of the physical form of one's discipline, one feels qualified, as a representative of the standard of the tradition, to engage in collaboration with individuals of other cultures, systems, and languages. Is typically a written treatise, but may take other forms.

Part III
Foundations of Physical Practice

At the beginning of orthodox training, the physical body must undergo certain preparations—it must learn a specific language before it is able to speak. Before advanced movements can be learned, one must understand basic foundational rules of body posture, hand movement, footsteps, and stances. Employed together, they support unification of body and mind.

CHAPTER 10

The Sash

In the ba gua quan tradition that Gong Baotian passed down to Gong Baozai, the sash is tied in a manner that binds the midsection firmly at the waist. The effects of a sash tied in this manner are threefold.

First, it serves the purpose of keeping the internal organs from shaking excessively when the body is in motion. Thus wear and tear on the organs, and stress on related body areas associated with the organs, are reduced. For example, the liver organ is known to be associated with the tendons and the eyes; the kidney organs with the bones, joints, and the ears. In this way, ba gua quan incorporates principles of Chinese medicine.

Second, binding of the waist region promotes respiration into the abdomen in a way that does not cause excessive enlargement of the abdominal region.

Third, pressure by the sash around the umbilicus serves as a constant reminder for the practitioner to pull the four limbs in toward the center of the torso. Pulling in the abdomen, to stabilize the waist and pelvic region, is a core yogic maneuver of Yin Fu ba gua.

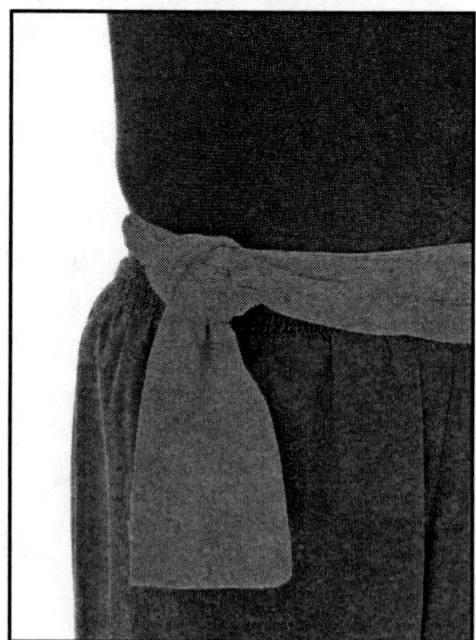

In traditional times, ba gua quan never employed a formal ranking system, nor were sash colors assigned. The ranking system has been implemented in present times as a means to give students some control over their personal development. The assignment of colored sashes with varying numbers of stripes, reflecting different levels of proficiency, adds organization and clarity to an otherwise amorphous learning experience. Traditionally, it was customary to keep the student, save the most dedicated followers, unaware as to as their progress or the extent of the system. In contrast, modern students should, from the very beginning, assume joint responsibility for their studies.

The sash categories are listed below. The red sash indicates beginner or disciple status; the black sash indicates teacher and master status. The gold sash is a symbolic honor awarded to a ba gua practitioner for achieving the ultimate rank of Grand Master.

Art of Discipleship

Red 1 – Red sash with one black stripe
Red 2 – Red sash with two black stripes
Red 3 – Red sash with three black stripes

Art of Teachership

Black 1 – Black sash with one red stripe
Black 2 – Black sash with two red stripes
Black 3 – Black sash with three red stripes
Black 4 – Black sash with four red stripes

Art of Mastership

Black 5 – Black sash with five red stripes
Black 6 – Black sash with six red stripes

Way of the Prophet or Saint

Black 7 – Black sash with seven red stripes
Black 8 – Black sash with eight red stripes; gold sash with eight black stripes

CHAPTER 11

Da Ba Duan Jin: Great Eight Brocades

Invented by the famous scholar General Yueh Fei (1103–1142 A.D.), Great Eight Brocades (*Da Ba Duan Jin*) has a long history as a simple yet effective health exercise. Many versions of this routine are currently practiced. Compared to more popular versions, the version taught by Gong Baozai bears the distinct quality of the Yin Fu ba gua style.

The hands and arms are drawn much tighter to the torso in the classic "sticking close to the body" (*tie shen*) fashion of Yin Fu ba gua that is required to sculpt the fascia to move the internal organs. Though some of the traditional names of Great Eight Brocades refer to organs and therapeutic benefits, the effect is of a more general nature than the specific targeting accomplished in ba gua's Eight Mother Palms practice.

This is an excellent warm-up routine to give the beginner an experience of the unique way that movement is executed in this practice.

THE EIGHT BROCADES

Opening posture: The opening posture is the same for all eight brocades.

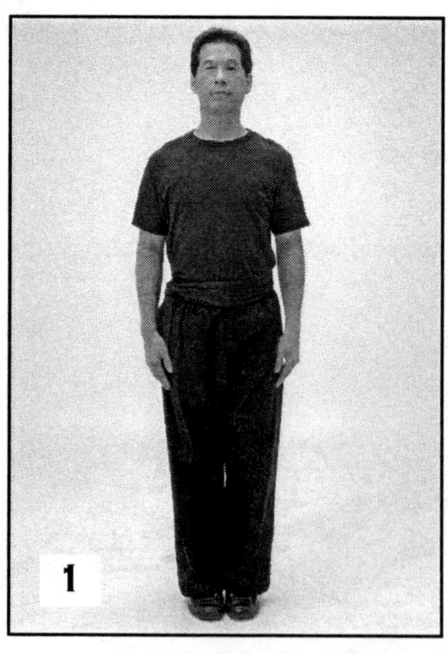

3

4

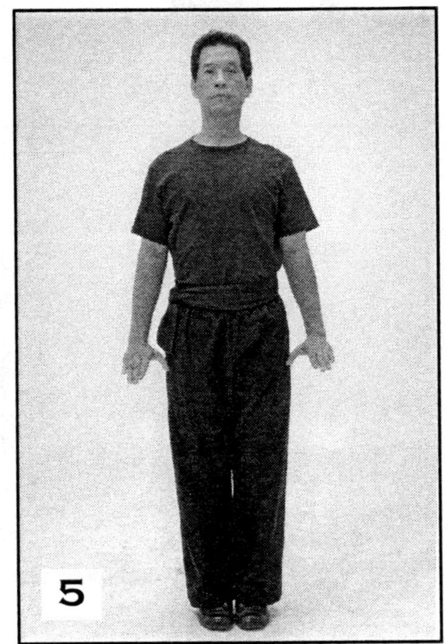
5

Brocade 1: *Liang shou qing tian li san jiao*
Two hands holding up heaven regulate the triple burner

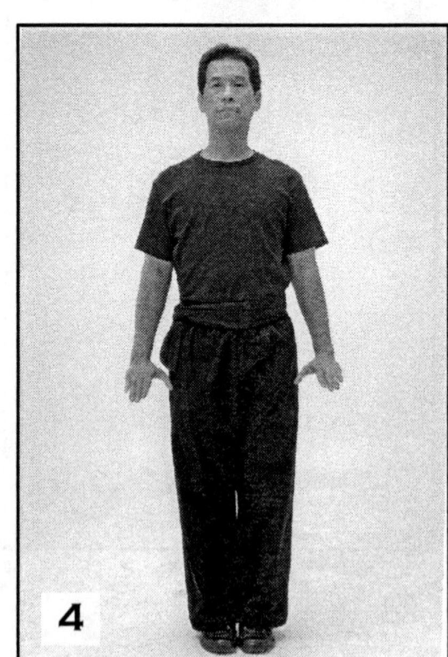

Brocade 2: *Zuo you kai gong si she diao*

Left and right drawing the bow to shoot the hawk

Brocade 3: *Tiao li pi wei dan ju shou*
Regulating spleen and stomach with single hand lifting

1

2

3

4

Brocade 4: *Wu lao qi shang hui hou qiao*

Curing the five fatigues and seven sicknesses by backward glancing

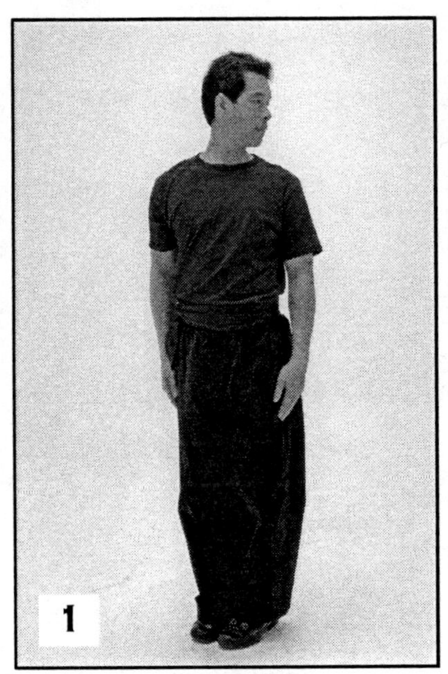

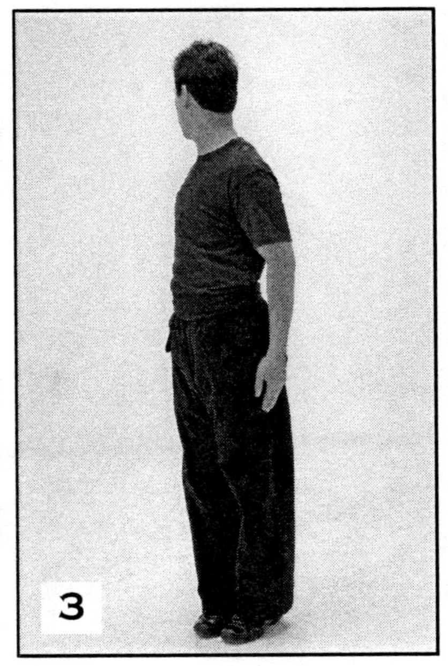

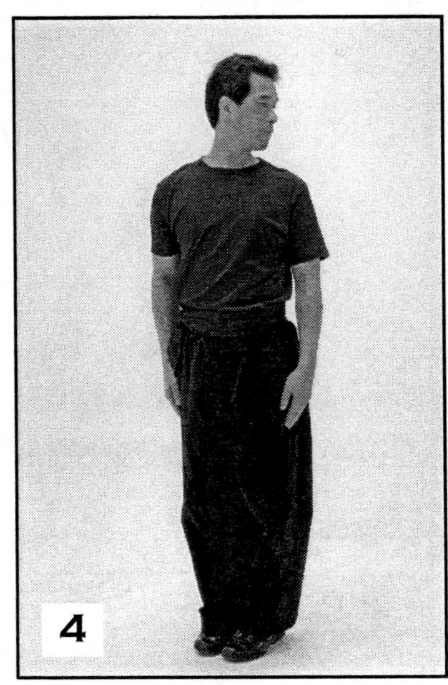

Brocade 5: *Yao tou bai wei chu xin huo*
Shaking the head and wagging the tail to rid heart fire

Phase 2
1

2

3

4

5

6

7

8

9

10

Brocade 6: *Bei hou qi dian bai bing xiao*

Falling from the seven cervical vertebrae down the back rids the hundred diseases

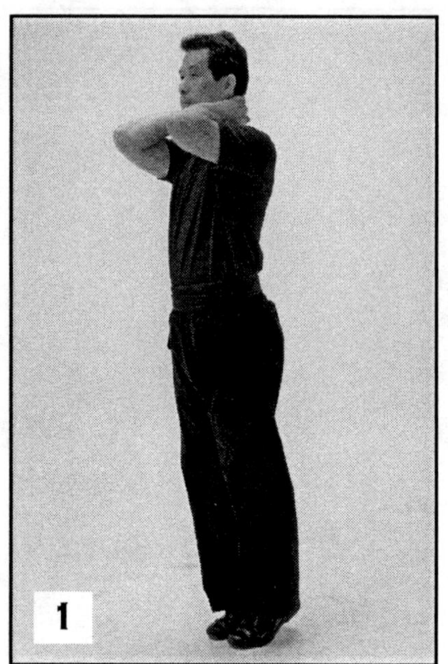

Brocade 7: *Zhuan quan nu mu zeng qi li*

Drilling the fists with angry eyes to increase qi and strength

Brocade 8: *Shuang shou pan zu gu sheng yao*
Two hands hanging from the feet to solidify kidneys and waist

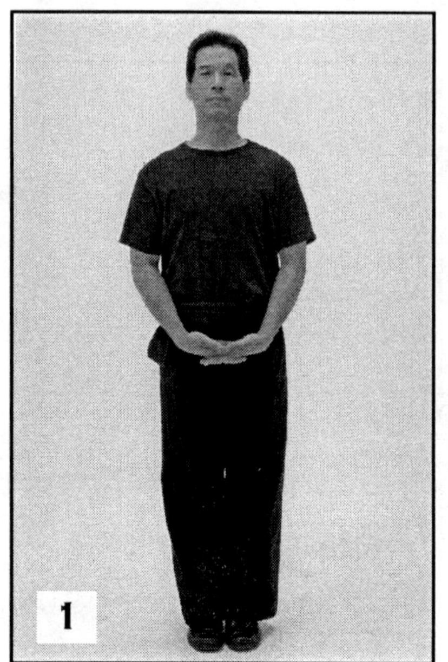

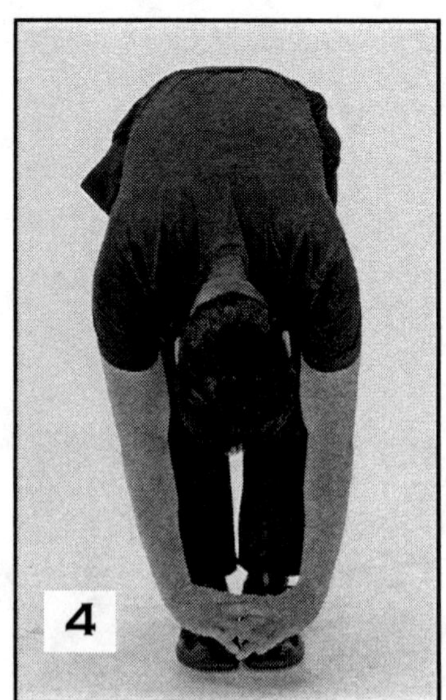

5

6

7

8

9

Closing posture: The closing posture is the same for all eight brocades.

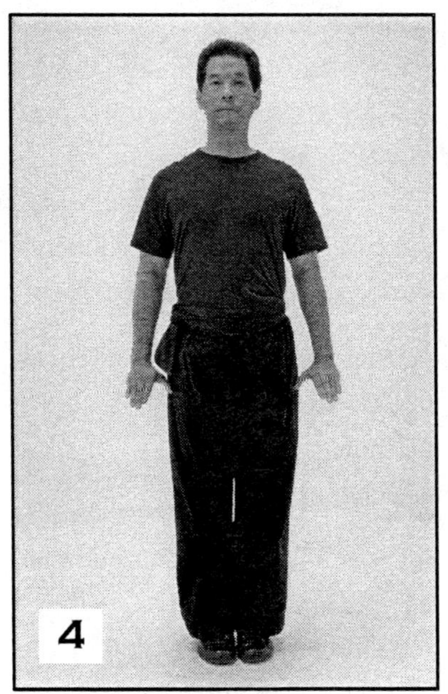

CHAPTER 12

Basic Stance Training

The martial arts stance is the foundation upon which all other development rests. Without a proper stance, power cannot be generated from the feet, and strength transmitted through the hands can never be refined beyond brute force. It is therefore mandatory that during the foundational phase of training, one endeavors with full mind, body, and spirit to understand the principles of correct physical posture.

The body's physical frame both reflects and supports inner development. The foundation for upright character lies in achieving proper outer posture and presentation. Such an intricate association between inner and outer illustrates the sophistication of orthodox systems. The mind foremost needs to be quiet and inwardly still, enabling posture alone to direct and guide the qi through the channels. This frees the attention to focus on social responsibility and ethical conduct.

Basic stance training is designed to prepare the body for the rigors of martial arts practice. The total number of stances employed in martial arts are many, but in this system three are generally considered most rudimentary. They are the horse riding posture (*qi ma shi*), forward arrow stance (*deng gong bu*), and containing opportunities stance (*han ji bu*).

In Yin Fu ba gua practice, grasping the principle of movement is more important than rigid adherence to a form. To guide a principled inquiry, the ancients passed down the following six correspondences:

Three outer correspondences:
Hand and foot
Elbow and knee
Shoulder and hip

Three inner correspondences:
Heart and mind
Mind and qi
Qi and strength

The three outer correspondences are exercised in basic stance training. More advanced methods are needed to cultivate the three inner correspondences.

Basic Three-Stance Sequence

The following pages present the entire three-stance sequence, illustrating the most essential principles of body mechanics and movement. Once students are familiar with this sequence, they should be free to perform it in any order, paying close attention to fluidity within the transitions from one posture to the next. The sequence is presented in this order:

- opening
- horse riding posture
- left forward arrow stance
- right forward arrow stance
- left han ji bu
- right han ji bu
- horse riding posture
- closing

Opening
1

2

3

4

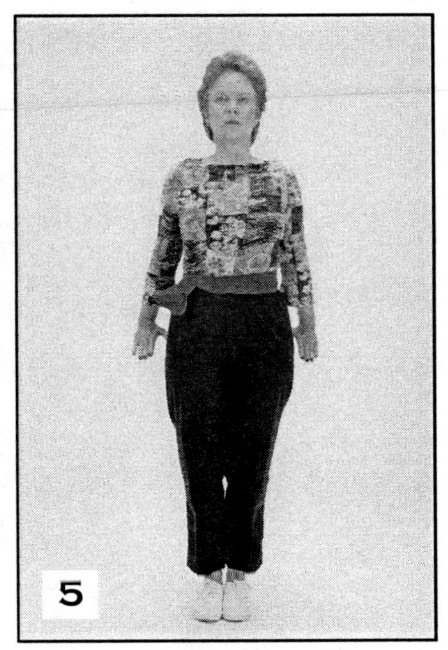
5

Horse riding posture
1

2

3A

3B

Left forward arrow stance
1

2

3

Right forward arrow stance

Left han ji bu
1

2

3A

3B

Right han ji bu
1

2A

2B

Horse riding posture
1

2

3A

3B

Closing
1

2

3

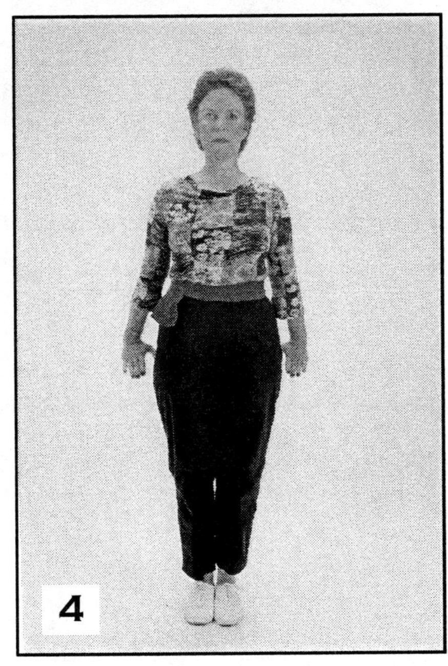
4

CHAPTER 13

Elements of Footwork

Ba gua quan is well known for its breakdown of the walking step into two components: the "open step" (*bai bu*) and the "closed step" (*cou bu*). They are an elaboration on the normal way we walk, made into a training exercise to develop the ability to quickly maneuver during hand-to-hand combat.

While more extensive treatment of Yin Fu ba gua's famed stepping methods is presented in other works by the author, the two most essential are illustrated here.

BAI "OPEN" STEP

For each progression from Level 1 to Level 3, note the increased distance between the feet.

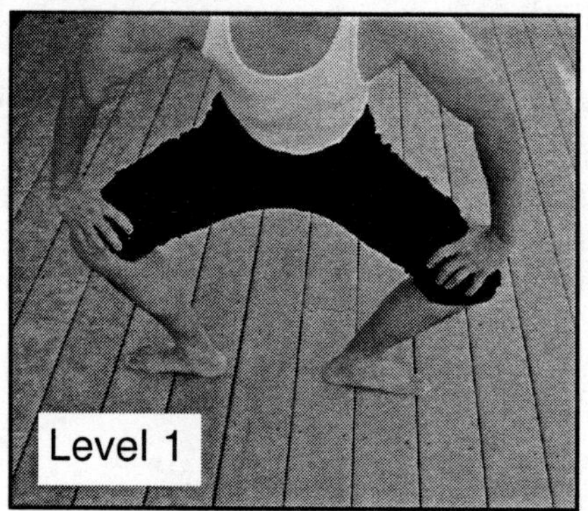

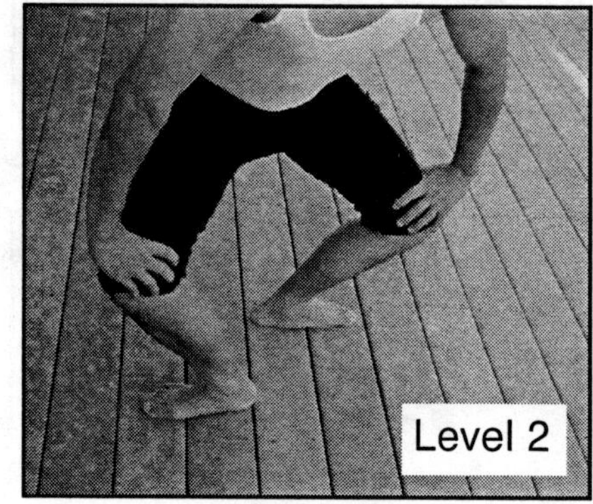

Comparison of little horse riding and normal horse riding stances: In both, the chest is raised, abdomen is pulled in, and shoulders are rolled back and down.

Characteristic Leg Maneuvers

Characteristic of this style's leg maneuvers is the "closed groin" (*jin dang*), which both protects the vital organs and keeps the qi energy lifted up and sealed in.

Kidney palm's White Tiger Straddles Road (*bai hu zhi lu*)

3

Bai Step
4

5

Cou Step
6

CHAPTER 14

Basic Yin Fu Ba Gua Quan Hand Positions

Characteristic of the hand positions of this style are the closed fingers, which promote refined mental focus and can be used to strike or grasp pressure points.

THE YIN FU BA GUA QUAN OX TONGUE PALM (NIU SHE ZHANG)

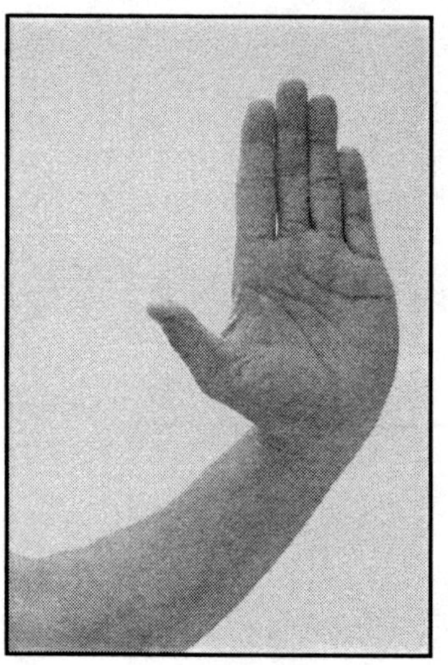

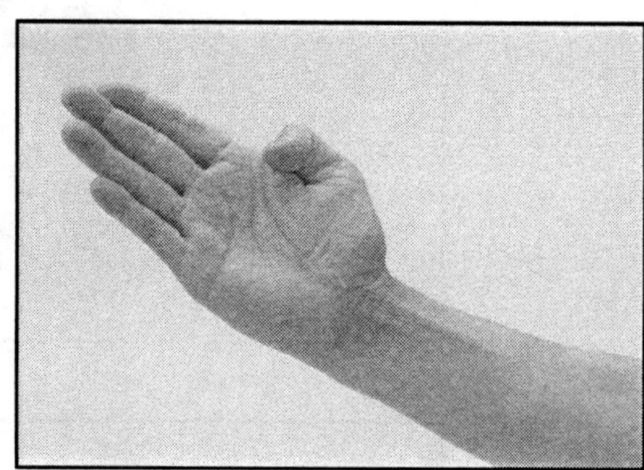

THE YIN FU BA GUA QUAN FIST

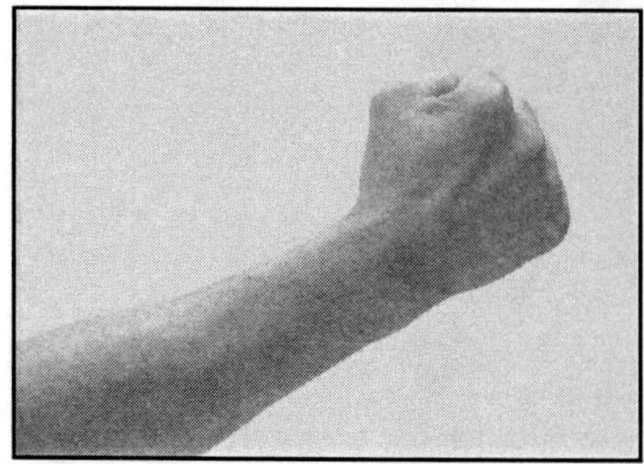

APPENDIXES

Traditional Chinese Origins of the Universe Theory

This theory constitutes the basic framework upon which the ba gua quan system is based, integrating Chinese medicine, mysticism, and martial arts.

Void *Wu ji:* (stillness) pre-heaven

Somethingness *Tai ji:* (movement; something) post-heaven, self-renewal

Two Appearances *Liang yi:* two limbs, duality, left/right, above/below, inside/outside, front/back

Four Images *Si xiang:* four limbs, four inner organs, four outer organs, four cardinal directions, four oblique directions

Eight Trigrams *Ba gua:* eight directions, eight dimensions of a complete self-inquiry

Sixty-four Hexagrams *Bian hua wu chong:* Unlimited Changeability; 108 permutations of the eight basic methods.

Root Internal and External Forms of the Yin Fu Ba Gua Quan System

ROOT EXTERNAL FORMS

- Basic root stances
- Single Changing Palm *Dan huan zhang* aka *Tui zhang* (Pushing Palm)
- Sixty-four Posture Cannon Fist *Pao chui* aka *Tong bi luo han quan* (Opening Shoulders and Arms Lohan Fist)

Eight Trigram Palace Fists

Chien Palace Fist	*Chien gong quan* (not transmitted)
Kan Palace Fist	*Kan gong quan*
Gen Palace Fist	*Gen gong quan* (not transmitted)
Zhen Palace Fist	*Zhen gong quan*
Shun Palace Fist	*Shun gong quan* (not transmitted)
Li Palace Fist	*Li gong quan aka Shi ba lo han quan* (18 Lohan Fist)
Kun Palace Fist	*Kun gong quan*
Dui Palace Fist	*Dui gong quan*

ROOT INTERNAL FORMS

- The Art of Two Appearances (*Liang yi zhi shu*)
- Four Images Fist (*Si xiang quan*)
- Eight Palm Fist (*Ba zhang quan* aka *Ba gua zhang, Ba zhang*)
- Eight Mother Palms (*Ba mu zhang*), includes Double Changing Palm (*Shuang huan zhang*)

Classical Internal Weapons

- Ba gua Sword (*Ba gua jian*)
- Ba gua Yin Plum Blossom Spear (*Ba gua mei hua yin qiang*)
- Ba gua Yang Plum Blossom Spear (*Ba gua mei hua yang qiang*)

Classical External Weapons

- Ba gua Broadsword (*Ba gua dao*)
- Ba gua Staff (*Ba gua gun*)

Advanced Practice Integrating Internal and External

- Eight Standing Meditations (*Zhan ba mu zhang*)
- Eight Palm Fist Blended into Eight Mother Palms
- Sixty-four Posture Cannon Fist Blended into Eight Mother Palms
- Latter Steps of Ba Gua Meditation (*Hou qi ba gua*)

Auxiliary

- One- and two-person forms, exercises, and weapons routines (all listed in Ranking System Chart)

Appendix 3

Pao Chui Footstep Map

Pao Chui is to be practiced according to the footstep map below, drawn on the post-heaven diagram. The main objective of this form is to "use softness to overcome hardness." Once the form becomes second nature, the various methods of change for self-defense can be studied.

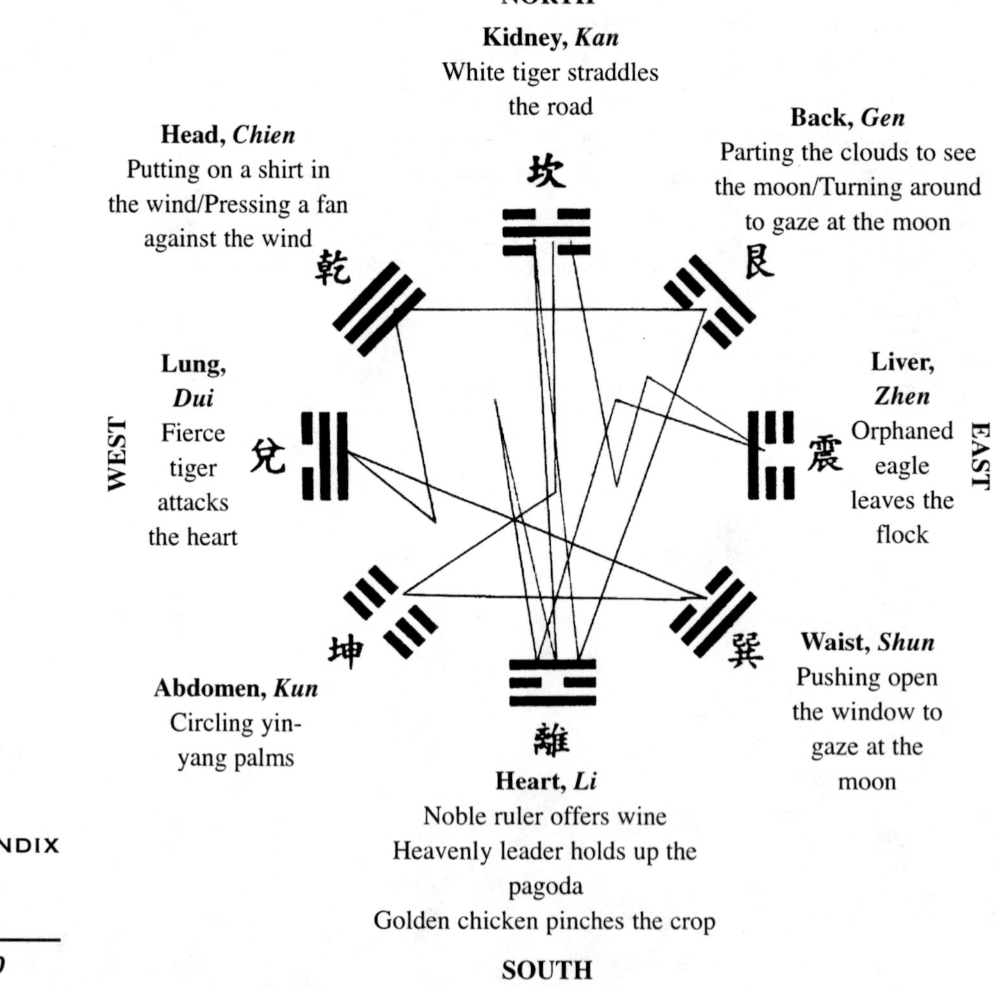

List of Pao Chui Movements

Pao Chui, or Cannon Fist, is composed of 64 movements. When including yin-yang changes, there is a total of 108 palms.

Translated by Dr. Michael Guen

Commencement posture (*Qi shou shi*)

1. Left brush support strike (*Zuo tiao da*)
2. Right brush support strike (*You tiao da*)
3. Thrust out right fist (*Chu you quan*)
4. Right brush support strike (*You tiao da*)
5. Thrust out right palm (*Chu you zhang*)
6. White crane flashes its wings (*Bai he liang chi*)
7. Cutting yin palm (*Qie yin zhang*)
8. Horizontally pushing eight horses (*Heng tui ba ma*)
9. Pulling the horse to the trough (*La ma gui cao*)
10. Breaking palm (*Cuo zhang*)
11. Yin fist (*Yin chui*)
12. Scissors palm (*Jian cha zhang*)
13. Overturning heaven palm (*Fan tian zhang*)
14. Pulling and pushing the horse (*La ma sung ma*)
15. Pressing on the summit of Mount Tai (*Tai shan ya ding*)
16. Noble ruler shackles right elbow (*You ba wang kun zhou*)
17. Noble ruler shackles left elbow (*Zuo ba wang kun zhou*)
18. Golden chicken stands on one leg (*Jin ji du li*)
19. Windmill palm (*Feng lun zhang*)
20. Left oblique palm (*Zuo pian zhang*)
21. Circling yin-yang palms (*Pan shun yin yang zhang*)
22. Left twisting dragon (*Zuo pan long*)
23. Whirlwind palm (*Xuan feng zhang*)
24. Offering the elbow (*Xian zhou*)

25. Reverse body palm (*Fan shen zhang*)
26. Double winds clapping the ears (*Shuang feng guan er*)
27. Pushing open the window to gaze at the moon (*Tui chuang wang yue*)
28. Leaning against the mountain palm (*Kao shan zhang*)
29. Fierce tiger attacks the heart (*Er hu dao xin*)
30. Left brush support strike (*Zuo tiao da*)
31. White ape zigzags left around rope (*Zuo bai yuan guai suo*)
32. White ape zigzags right around rope (*You bai yuan guai suo*)
33. Right brush support strike (*You tiao da*)
34. White ape zigzags right around rope (*You bai yuan guai suo*)
35. White ape zigzags left around rope (*Zuo bai yuan guai suo*)
36. Folding fists (*Die chui*)
37. Left folding fists (*Zuo die chui*)
38. Right spinning fists (*You xuan chui*)
39. Reverse body fists right (*You fan shen chui*)
40. Pressing a fan against the wind (*Ying feng tui shan*)
41. Putting on a shirt in the wind (*Ying feng chuan xiu*)
42. Raising the hem with a fluid step (*Xun bu liao yi*)
43. Parting the clouds to see the moon (*Bo yun jian yue*)
44. Turning around to gaze at the moon (*Hui tou wang yue*)
45. Penetrating heart palm (*Chuan xin zhang*)
46. Single colliding palm (*Dan zhuang zhang*)
47. Traversing one mountain after another (*Er ji dan shan*)
48. Noble ruler offers wine (*Ba wang jing jiu*)
49. White tiger straddles the road (*Bai hu zhi lu*)
50. Capturing left elbow (*Zuo bao zhou*)
51. Capturing right elbow (*You bao zhou*)
52. Leaping up to chop at the tiger (*Tsuan tiao qie hu*)
53. Heavenly ruler holds up the pagoda (*Tian wang tuo ta*)
54. Crossing fists (*Shi dz chui*)
55. Folding fists (*Die chui*)
56. Right folding fists (*You die chui*)
57. Left spinning fists (*Zuo xuan chui*)
58. Reverse body fists left (*Zou fan shen chui*)
59. Golden chicken pinches the crop (*Jin ji nie su*)

60. Circling phoenix returns to nest (*Feng huang xuan wo*)
61. Orphaned eagle leaves the flock (*Gu ying chu chun*)
62. Mystical dragon whips its tail (*Qing long bai wei*)
63. Double colliding palms (*Shuang zhuang zhang*)
64. Playful magpie darts through branches (*Xi chue chuan zhi*)
    Closing posture (*Shou shi*)

Appendix 5

Pao Chui Trigram Palace Names

Heart, *Li*
Noble ruler offers wine
Heavenly leader holds up the pagoda
Golden chicken pinches the crop

Lung, *Dui*
Fierce tiger attacks the heart

Liver, *Zhen*
Orphaned eagle leaves the flock

Kidney, *Kan*
White tiger straddles the road

Head, *Chien*
Putting on a shirt in the wind/Pressing a fan against the wind

Back, *Gen*
Parting the clouds to see the moon/Turning around to gaze at the moon

Waist, *Shun*
Pushing open the window to gaze at the moon

Abdomen, *Kun*
Circling yin-yang palms

Eight Mother Palms Diagram

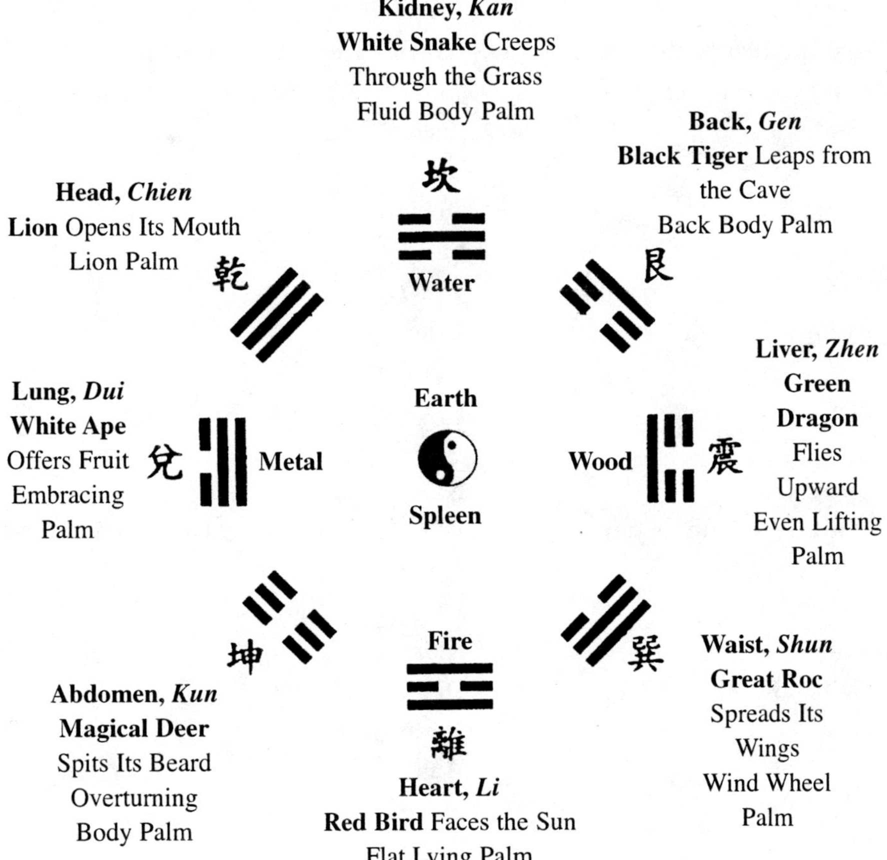

APPENDIX 7

The Eight Mother Palms and Their Characteristics

FOUR INNER PALMS

Heart, *Li*
Red Bird Faces the Sun
Dan feng chao yang
Flat Lying Palm
Heart
Qi blood
South
Fire
Rising
Blood vessels
Tongue–taste

Liver, *Zhen*
Green Dragon Flies Upward
Qing long fei sheng
Even Lifting Palm
Liver
Qi blood
East
Wood
Expanding
Tendons
Eyes–sight

Lung, *Dui*
White Ape Offers Fruit
Bai yuan xian guo
Embracing Palm
Lung
Qi blood
West
Metal
Congealing
Skin
Nose–smell

Kidney, *Kan*
White Snake Creeps Through the Grass
Bai she fu cao
Fluid Body Palm
Kidney
Qi blood
North
Water
Falling
Bones/marrow
Ears–hearing

Four Outer Palms

Head, *Chien*
Lion Opens Its Mouth
Shi zi zhang cou
Lion Palm
Head
Muscle tendons
Northwest

Waist, *Shun*
Great Roc Spreads Its Wings
Da peng zhan chi
Wind Wheel Palm
Waist
Muscle tendons
Southeast

Back, *Gen*
Black Tiger Leaps from the Cave
Hei hu chu dong
Back Body Palm
Back
Muscle tendons
Northeast

Abdomen, *Kun*
Magical Deer Spits Its Beard
Chi lin tu xu
Overturning Body Palm
Abdomen
Muscle tendons
Southwest

Inner and Outer Palms Correspondences

Heart with Head

Lung with Back

Liver with Waist

Kidney with Abdomen

Changing Palm in Four Postures

Green Dragon Wags Its Tail (Green Dragon Turns Its Head) *Qing long bai wei* *(Qing long fan shou)*	Even Lifting Palm (liver)
Giant Python Turns Over Its Body *Da mang fan shen*	Back Body Palm (back)
Black Bear Reaches Out Its Paw *Hei xiong tan zhua*	Wind Wheel Palm (waist)
White Snake Coils Its Body *Bai she chan shen*	Flat Lying Palm (heart)
Fifth Posture Evasion Palm in One Move *Tang zhang yi shi*	Fluid Body Palm (kidney)

Appendix 10

Ba Zhang Quan (Eight Palm Fist) Postures

Order of appearance in the form:

Red Bird Faces the Sun	heart, *li*
Black Tiger Leaps from the Cave	back, *gen*
Great Roc Spreads Its Wings	waist, *shun*
Lion Opens Its Mouth	head, *chien*
White Ape Offers Fruit	lung, *dui*
Green Dragon Flies Upward	liver, *zhen*
White Snake Creeps Through the Grass	kidney, *kan*
Magical Deer Spits Its Beard	abdomen, *kun*

Appendix 11

Proper Student Protocol

Proper protocol gives the student a chance to exercise the fundamental discipleship-level skills of following and listening, in the support of the teacher and the spirit of the community. While adherence to proper protocol reflects the student's understanding and assimilation of relationships and boundaries, it also builds self-awareness, integrity, self-discipline, and a more stable and orderly community. The student is expected to abide by these guidelines:

- Conduct oneself semi-formally, combining western and Asian custom.
- Employ basic courtesies, such as being prompt to class and not leaving prematurely.
- Pay tuition and fees on time.
- Notify the teacher beforehand if one will miss class or an appointment.
- Volunteer to maintain neatness of the physical space.
- Take part in tea/water preparation.
- Bow at the waist when leaving the school (*guan*).
- Show proper respect by not talking or acting in ways that disrupt class harmony and continuity.

How the student conducts him or herself with the teacher differs when inside and outside the class setting. In class, proper formality and respect shall be shown toward the teacher and classmates. Outside of class, no formal behavior is expected, except that which naturally extends from the heart. Deference to a teacher is not a sign of weakness or inferiority but, on the contrary, is a worthwhile foundational attitude that is continually nurtured throughout one's life.

Should practitioners of Junior Instructor, Black 1, rank or higher wish to attend another teacher's class, or a mind-body discipline class outside the Yin Fu ba gua system, it is their obligation to discuss this with their primary teacher. This policy does not apply to students at the red sash stage, who are not expected to express as high a degree of commitment.

APPENDIX 12

The Character Diary

The character diary, kept by both instructors and practitioners, is an effective tool for the process of growth through leadership. By daily recording one's experiences in a character diary, one gains awareness of the correct use of both personal and social energy.

Beginning in the early phase of black sash training, one assumes responsibility for the growth of others. The curriculum is designed to minimize competitive interaction between teacher and student. Thus begins the emphasis on and trend toward service.

Leadership as a form of self-sufficiency requires ethical handling of relationships. Taming the natural survival instinct (*sheng cun jing zheng*) is vital for expansion and growth. When a teacher's survival instinct is combined with the capacity to listen and yield, and therefore see the bigger picture, one's character is balanced.

The character diary expedites leadership training by revealing otherwise unconscious, interfering, and undisclosed social dynamics. It is a demonstration of faith in one's worth and divinity beyond any credential. The diary requires self-examination with a critical review of past actions. Such rigorous disclosing of one's inner process by the teacher to his or her teacher, and to his or her students, is an act of openness and trust.

The procedure will entail a regular review, arranged by private appointment, with one's teacher. The teacher will also set aside a regular time to share discoveries with and receive feedback from students.

Appendix 13

Testing Philosophy and Procedures

Formal testing is an opportunity for the practitioner to receive feedback from the teacher and possibly other higher-ranking instructors. In applying for testing at a certain rank, the practitioner asserts achievement, based on self-assessment, of a level of proficiency in the required curriculum. At the completion of testing, the accuracy of the self-assessment is revealed. In this way, a practitioner is given a tool for sharpening and verifying the ability to discriminate.

This testing philosophy also provides for incremental evaluation of the practitioner's progress in the physical requirements of the system and recognition of true accomplishment of character.

The testing formality begins with all applicants lining up according to rank (and then seniority). This can be in either a circle or line form, as determined by the number of applicants and the physical space. Led by the highest-ranking instructor, who is at the front of the group, facing the applicants, an opening ceremonial bow is performed, acknowledging the ancestors of the lineage, the senior instructors, senior students, and practitioners of the community.

The demonstration of required capabilities begins with the most basic exercise required for the lowest rank being tested. At the level of red sash, all testing is done as a group. This inculcates an awareness of community spirit. Advancement is not exclusively an individual achievement but an achievement of the entire community.

Beginning with the rank of Black 1, Junior Instructor, testing becomes more individualized. Performance is generally evaluated one candidate at a time. Two-person applications, sparring, weapons, and some circle-walking demonstrations are exceptions.

Testing for advancement to higher ranks, Black 2, Associate Instructor, through Black 7, Senior Master, shall be performed in front of a panel of three instructors ranked at least one level higher than the rank being applied for. For example, a panel of three instructors at a minimum rank of Black 4,

Senior Instructor, shall evaluate the performance of an applicant applying for the rank of Black 3, Instructor. When this is not possible, testing to establish initial rank shall be performed by the head instructor. Testing for the ranks Red 1 through Red 3 may be performed at the discretion of an instructor of rank Black 2, Associate Instructor, or higher. Evaluation for advancement to the rank of Black 8, Grand Master, shall be performed by a panel of Grand Masters, when possible.

At the test, each applicant will be called to demonstrate by the testing instructor. The applicant waits for permission to begin the demonstration. All other applicants wait quietly, out of the way of the testing.

Taking advantage of a unique learning experience, applicants not currently performing shall pay close attention to both the individual who is performing the demonstration and the instructor. In this way, the individual who is performing remains connected with the community. The community, in turn, gains an awareness of proper execution in the testing environment, as the private evaluation leads to discrimination. The many levels of awareness that the testing instructor must apply are demonstrated in the evaluation of an applicant's performance.

During testing, if an applicant is unable to complete a form or technique, or wishes to repeat his or her performance, the applicant may request permission to start over. Permission is granted at the discretion of the testing instructor.

At the conclusion of all testing, the highest-ranking instructor will call for a lineup. Another bow is then performed to the testing instructors.

APPENDIX 14

Fees Structure

To maintain balance in the teacher-student relationship, some form of energy exchange is necessary. In the early phases of the relationship, this exchange is characterized by the teacher investing time and energy in creating and holding a learning space, on several levels, on behalf of the student. In exchange, the student makes a partial repayment in the form of money.

At later stages, payment for individual lessons may be substituted with other energetic exchanges. Projects for the teacher and the community, as well as other ways of maintaining the energetic balance, may be employed. This is at the discretion of the teacher.

Monetary payments will also flow from teachers to their instructor. This provides one mechanism for the partial repayment of the enormous investment an upper-level teacher has made in his or her students.

The fee structure for any individual class is at the discretion of the instructor for that class, recognizing his or her free will and right to determine the form of compensation. Any waiver of fees should be done with the recognition of the effect such an act has on the higher-level instructors and, as such, it should be discussed with them. This is done not so much for permission but to obtain agreement and understanding that a proper application of the underlying principles has been made.

It is recommended that instructors base their fees, in part, on their rank. This process recognizes that the learning experience provided by a higher-ranking instructor will move a student along in a more powerful manner.

In this spirit of appreciation, twenty percent of all fees shall be set aside and paid by each instructor to his or her teacher. The only exception is at the Black 8 rank, where no percentage to one's teacher is paid.

This process continues at each level, from student to teacher, so that payments continue to flow upward, until it reaches the highest-ranked teacher in the system. At each level an instructor adds all payments from his or her own students, plus twenty percent of all payments made by instructors under his or her supervision, in calculating the amount to submit to his or her own instructor. Payments are to be forwarded on a quarterly basis.

The following chart represents a sample fee schedule. *Adjustments should be made by the teacher according to regional economics and the disparity in earning capacity for women and other groups.*

RECOMMENDED FEE SCHEDULE

Instructor Rank	Group Instruction (per class)	Individual Instruction (per hour)
Black 1 – Junior Instructor	$10	$25
Black 2 – Associate Instructor	$10	$30
Black 3 – Instructor	$10	$35
Black 4 – Senior Instructor	$10	$40
Black 5 – Junior Master	$12	$50
Black 6 – Master	$15	$75
Black 7 – Senior Master	Discretionary	Discretionary
Black 8 – Grand Master	Discretionary	Discretionary

TEST FEES

In recognition of the energetic resources required by an instructor to evaluate the performance of an applicant for rank advancement, and to maintain a proper test environment, the following sample testing fees shall apply.

Rank	Fee
Red 1	$25
Red 2	$25
Red 3	$25
Black 1	$500
Black 2	$625
Black 3	$750
Black 4	$875
Black 5	$1,000
Black 6	$1,500
Black 7	$2,000
Black 8	No fee

References

Pa Kua Chang Journal, Volume 4, No.5, July/August 1994, pp. 3–14.

Ba Gua Quan: Foundational Training, He Jing-Han, Lion Books, Taipei, 2003.

Ba Gua Quan Ji Chu: Foundations of Ba Gua Quan compiled by He Jinghan (in Chinese), Yi Wen Publishing Co., Taiwan, 2000.

Understanding the I Ching, Helmut Wilhelm and Richard Wilhelm, Princeton, Bollingen Series, 1995.

I Ching or *Book of Changes,* Richard Wilhelm and Cary F. Baynes, 3rd Ed. Princeton, Bollingen Series, 1967.